Weather

by Jack Fleming*

Contents

Chapter 1 What is Weather? 7

    The Greenhouse Effect 8
    Convection – Heat and Air Movement 10
   Humidity – Water in the Atmosphere 12

Chapter 2. An Ocean of Air 14

    Layers of the Atmosphere 15
    The Troposphere 16
    The Stratosphere 19
    The Ionosphere 19
    The Exosphere 19
    Composition of Dry Air 22

Chapter 3. The Water Cycle - Water in the Atmosphere and Heat 24

Chapter 4. Clouds 28

  High Altitude Clouds 30

  Middle Clouds 34

  Low Clouds 36

Chapter 5. Precipitation - Rain, Snow, Ice, Frost, and Dew 42

   Rain 44
   Rainbows 46
   Snow 49
   Hail 50

Frost 53
Glaze 53
Sleet 54

Chapter 6. The Motion of the Earth 56

Seasons 56
Summer 57
Experiment: 58

Chapter 7. Measuring and Recording Weather 59

Air Pressure Measurements 59
Temperature Measurements 60
Wind Direction 62
Wind Speed 63
Rain Gauge 64
Relative Humidity 65
Weather Satellites 71

Chapter 8. High Pressure, Low Pressure 74

High-Pressure Wind Velocities 75
Low-Pressure Formation 76

Chapter 9. Wind 78

Planetary Winds 79
Secondary Winds 80
Monsoons 81
Regional Winds 81
Beaufort Wind Scale 83

Chapter 10. Fronts 86

Equatorial and Polar Fronts 87
Warm Fronts 88
Stationary Front 89
Cold Fronts 89
Occluded Fronts 90

Chapter 11. Storms - Thunderstorms, Hurricanes, Blizzards, and Tornadoes 92

Rainstorms 94
  Snowstorms 94
  Thunderstorms 97
  Lightning and Thunder 101
  Floods 104
  Tornadoes 104
  Hurricanes 110

Chapter 12. Forecasting the Weather 115

  Predicting Weather by Observation 116
  Using a Barometer and Wind Direction to Predict Weather 117

  Use of a Barometer –119

  The barometer has been in use since the 19th century. Forecasting the weather using the measurements over a period of time permitted the early meteorologist a tool to use in forecasting and recording the weather. They've noticed that the faster the change in air pressure had occurred, the faster the change in the weather occurred. Farmers especially needed this information to maintain their crops. If the pressure was of a 'low' pressure drop, they knew that rain is on the way. They also knew that if the 'high' pressure rise occurred, that fair weather conditions were approaching.119

  Weather and its effect on humans 120

  Can Humans Control the Weather? 121

  Forecasting 122

  Meteorologist 123

  Types of Meteorology 124

  Hydrometeorology 124
  The study of the distribution of gases and radioactive aerosols in the atmosphere is called *nuclear meteorology*. 125

Environmental meteorology 125
How industrial pollution dispersion is physically and chemically impacted by the weather based on various temperatures, winds, humidity, and other weather conditions is called *environmental meteorology*.125
Renewable energy and meteorology 125
The mapping of wind power and solar radiation as a source of energy is a new field of meteorology. Renewable energy is a concern for many countries. 125

Numerical Weather Prediction 125

Today's Weather Tools 127

In case of severe or hazardous weather conditions, the national weather service will issue warnings and alerts. A warning or advisory alerts the public that potentially severe weather is near or imminent. A severe weather watch indicates that the danger is more than eminent. The danger has been observed and is within the broadcast area. Listeners would be urged to take shelter immediately or seek higher ground if flash flooding is expected.128

How are the Low Temperatures Calculated?128

Forecasting Air Traffic 129

Marine Weather Forecasting 131

Agriculture Industry Forecasting 132

Chapter 13. Climate 134

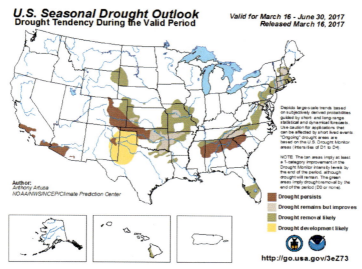

135

    Microclimatic Differences 135

    Climate Change 136

    Acid Rain 138

    Global Warming 138

    Ozone Layer 139

Chapter 14. Reading Weather Maps 144

    Surface Weather Maps 145

Chapter 15. Discoveries in Meteorology 148

    Early beliefs of weather prediction 149

    Historic Discoveries in Meteorology 151

Chapter 16. Terms 160

    NOAA Terms 165

    Terminology and Weather Symbols 165

Chapter 17. Greatest Annual Snowfalls in the U.S. 189

Chapter 18. Projects and badge requirements 191

Chapter 1 What is Weather?

Weather is defined as the short-term changes in temperature, humidity, rainfall, and barometric pressure in the atmosphere. **Weather** is the state of the atmosphere, the level of degree that it is hot or cold, whether the air is wet or dry, the movement of the air whether it is calm or stormy, and whether the air is clear or cloudy. Most weather occurs in the layer known as the troposphere, just below the next layer called the stratosphere. Weather refers to the daily temperature and precipitation activity. **Climate** is the statistical term of the atmospheric conditions over longer periods of time. Weather refers to the atmospheric weather conditions at the surface of the Earth. Where the atmosphere thins, weather does not exist. At the surface of the Earth, the atmosphere is dense and heavy. This is where the most changing weather, and sometimes violent weather occurs. Temperature changes are what primarily causes the changes in weather. The sun primarily influences the weather. Even though the sun is 93 million miles from Earth, it generates 126 trillion horsepower upon the Earth's surface every second. This is only about a half of one billionth of the energy produced by the sun. Most of the sun's energy is dissipated in space and only traces of the sun's energy reaches the surface of other planets. The transmission of the sun's energy is transmitted in the form of waves. Some of these waves are in the form of visible light and some are in the form of invisible waves.

43% of the sun's energy is absorbed by the surface of the Earth.

42% of the sun's energy is reflected back into space.

15% of the sun's energy is absorbed by earth's atmosphere.

The Earth is tilted on its axis in regarding to its orbital plane. Sunlight strikes the Earth at different angles during various times of the year. Temperatures can range between -40 degrees F (-40 C) to 100 degrees F at various times of the year. Changes within the Earth's orbit over the millennium has occurred, as a result, global climate change has been recorded. Not all of the sun's energy reaches the Earth's surface evenly. A cloud typically reflects 75% of the sunlight striking the Earth. The sunlight striking the Earth is absorbed or reflected at varying degrees. For instance, snow reflects about 75% of the sun's energy. Only 25% is absorbed in the snowy region. That is why the Earth's Polar Regions are cold. Dark forest absorbs 95% and that is converted to heat. These areas are ideal for plant growth.

Snow absorbs 25% of the sun's energy

Water absorbs 60% to 96% of the sun's energy. The absorption rate varies due to the angle of the sun.

Grassy fields absorb 80% to 90% of the sun's energy.

Plowed fields absorb 75% to 93% of the sun's energy.

Dense forest absorbs 95% of the sun's energy.

Dry sand absorbs 75% of the sun's energy.

The Greenhouse Effect

Short solar rays pass through the glass of a greenhouse. The rays are absorbed by the plants inside the greenhouse and are re-radiated as *long* heat rays. These long heat rays cannot pass through the glass and build up inside the greenhouse. This permits the heat to be retained inside the greenhouse on colder days. Of course, some heat is lost through conduction at the surface of the glass, however, the majority of the heat is retained inside the greenhouse.

The Earth's atmosphere acts like the greenhouse. As the solar radiation is reflected back into the atmosphere, the water vapor in the air traps the long solar radiation waves and the heat is retained by the Earth. The atmosphere allows the short solar waves to pass through, but the longer reflected waves remained trapped by the Earth's atmosphere.

The Earth's Atmosphere is a Thermostat

The atmosphere protects the Earth from getting too hot. It prevents too much radiation from striking the Earth's surface during the day while it screens out the dangerous waves bombarding the Earth. Like an insulation covering, it retains most of the heat from escaping the Earth at night.

Note that climate is characterized by hot, dry summers and cool, wet winters. A steppe is a dry grassland. Subarctic climates have continuous permafrost, which causes this area to be very cold with very little precipitation.

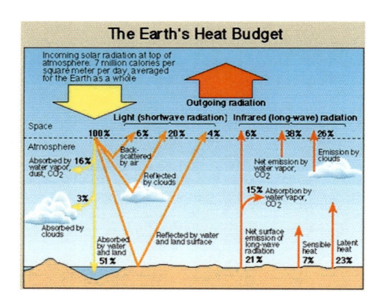

Convection – Heat and Air Movement

The warm earth heats the air. Heated air expands and rises up into the atmosphere. As the warmer air rises, cooler air flows beneath and replaces the risen air. The cooler air is then warmed and it also expands as it is heated and rises up into the atmosphere. This is called **convection**.

At the equator, the Earth receives more direct sunlight and is heated to the warm temperatures. The convection currents would rise and head toward the poles. However, due to the rotation of the Earth, the movements of the convection currents are different. Breezes and winds are caused by the convection currents. Depending on the land, convection currents behave differently. For instances, the mountains will absorb heat faster in the daytime and relieve the heat faster at night. Land absorbs heat faster than water mass does and will lose the heat faster at night than the water mass. The local wind behavior will be the result of the various land or water mass.

Humidity – Water in the Atmosphere

Most of the Earth, approximately 70% of the Earth's surface is covered with water. Therefore, water is always present in the air.

Humidity – Water content in the air is usually expressed as relative humidity.

Relative humidity is the amount of water that the air is holding as it is expressed as a percentage of the amount of water that the air could hold at a particular temperature. Warm air can hold more water than cold air. That is because of the space between the air molecules is greater. Warm air molecules bump into each other at a more excited rate, thus causing a greater space between the molecules of air. This allows more space for water molecules to occupy. The air at 86 degrees F. (30 C) can hold 30.4 grams of water per cubic meter. Whereas the lower air temperature of 68 degrees F. will only hold 17.3 grams of water per cubic meter. When the air reaches its saturation point (humidity max level) it will form rain. If the temperature is cold enough, the precipitation will fall as snow or ice.

Chapter 2. An Ocean of Air

The Earth's atmosphere extends approximately 1,500 miles (2,414 km) upwards from the Earth's surface. About 75% of the Earth's main gases are within the first ten miles (16 km) of the Earth's surface. The atmospheric layer closest to the ground contains primarily 78 percent nitrogen and about 21 percent oxygen. Argon gas is next to about 1 percent, and carbon dioxide at about 0.03 percent. Other gases appear in trace amounts. These gases are argon, neon, radon, helium, krypton, xenon, hydrogen, methane, nitrous oxide and ozone. Water vapor constantly varies in that within the first mile from the surface, water vapor can be at zero percent to 4 percent, depending on the location and other variables. Six miles from the surface, Ozone gas is found. This gas protects us from ultraviolet rays. Sixty-two miles from the Earth's surface is the darkness of space. If the Earth were perfectly still, the gases would separate where the heaviest gas would settle to the bottom and the other gases would rise according to their weight. But since the Earth is in constant motion, the gases are mixed in the same proportion from the surface to about 45 miles up. Because of gravity, this ocean of air has weight. At sea level, the ocean of air exerts 14.7 pounds of air pressure per square inch. The air pressure is exerted equally on all sides. This prevents objects from collapsing.

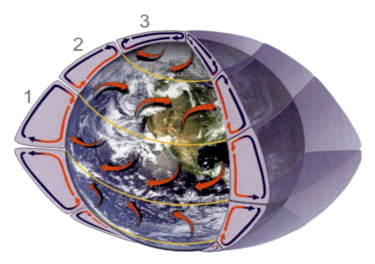

1 – Equatorial zone; 2 – Tropical zone; 3 – Polar zone

Layers of the Atmosphere – We live at the bottom of this ocean of air. Because of the density of air at the surface, life is able to survive. Only 500 miles from the surface, there are only 22 million molecules of air per cubic inch. At that level, 50 percent of the gas is hydrogen and 50 percent of the gas is helium. The atmosphere is divided into layers. The *heterosphere* is the upper portion which includes the thermosphere and ionosphere. The lower portion of the atmosphere is the *homosphere* which is further divided into other layers. The lowest section of the atmosphere is called the **troposphere**. This is the layer where life exists and where the weather takes place. The troposphere extends about 7 miles (11 km) from the surface. It is about 5 miles (8 km) thick at the poles and 10 miles (16 km) thick at the equator. Because the Earth is spinning, the Earth bulges 28 miles at the equator.

The next layer is the **stratosphere**. The gases have thinned at this altitude which is approximately 7 to 30 miles (11 to 48 km) from the surface. The next layer is the **ozonosphere** (ozone layer) which is located approximately 10 to 30 miles (16 to 48 km) from the surface. Although the ozone layer may be only a few inches thick, it is needed in that it protects us from the ultraviolet rays from the sun. This layer is sometimes referred to as the ionosphere because this is where the electrified (ionized) particles reflect long radio waves back to Earth.

The next layer is the **mesosphere**. The temperatures drop dramatically at this level. The mesosphere is 30 to 55 miles (48 to 88 km) from the surface of the Earth. The next layer is called the **thermosphere**. Because of the sun's rays, the temperature can rise to more than 1,800 degrees. The thermosphere is located 55 to 435 miles (85 to 700 km) from the Earth's surface. The last layer is called the **exosphere**. This final layer is 435 miles (700 km) above sea level.

The Troposphere – This is the layer where almost all of our weather occurs. This is the layer where the clouds form. The air is heated by the contact with the Earth. The warm air rises and is replaced by cooler air. Horizontal winds are created by vertical wind currents. Water that has evaporated from the surface is infused with the warm air. As the air rises, it cools and the water vapor condenses and clouds are formed.

Compression of a gas creates heat, while the expansion of a gas creates cooling. The heat source for the troposphere is the sun. It heats up the surface and causes the air to warm, expand, and rise. As the air rises and expands, it cools because the pressure is less. When air ascends over a mountain, it cools. As the air descends on the other side of the mountain, the air begins to compress. The rising and falling of air and the temperature change is called **adiabatic warming** or cooling. One example would be on the eastern slope of the Rocky Mountains. When the Chinook winds occur, the temperatures can rise from -6 degrees to 37 degrees in 15 minutes.

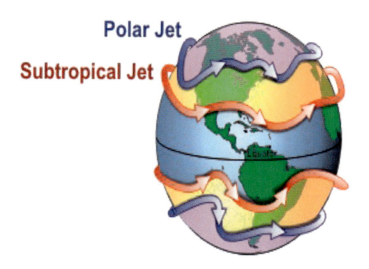

The Jet Stream and Tropopause – The tropopause is the area that marks the end of the troposphere and the start of the stratosphere. This layer is not continuous from the poles to the equator. The tropopause overlaps each layer proceeding it. Where the layers overlap, it forms what is known as the **jet stream**. The jet stream is tubular in a structure where one lengthy tube is encased by other lengthy tubes of very high winds. The winds generally are from the west and proceed easterly. The jet stream is from

20,000 to 40,000 feet above sea level. The artic tropopause and the extratropical tropopause are a result of the extreme temperature contrast.

During World War II, B-29 pilots discovered the jet stream while flying toward Japan from the Marianna Islands. The reported prevailing winds at an extreme speed. The four-mile high jet stream is usually about 300 miles wide. At the core of the jet stream, wind speeds are about 100 miles per hour in the winter and about 50 miles an hour in the summer. The wind speeds of the jet stream decrease from the core. There are three major jet streams. One over Canada, one over the United States, and one over the subtropics.

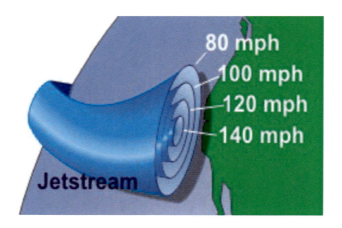

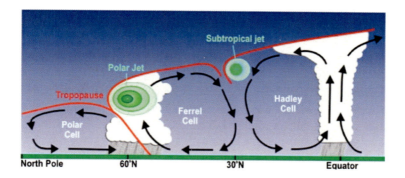

The Stratosphere – The stratosphere extends fifty miles from the troposphere. It is a uniformed layer with little or no vertical air movement. The temperature slightly rises near the top of the layer. Often, jet aircraft leave a trail of condensed fine ice crystals because the moisture from their jet fuel had condensed.

The Ionosphere – Extending 650 miles beyond the stratosphere is the ionosphere. The scattered air particles are ionized because of the loss of an electron. The constant hail of cosmic rays from space causes the ionization. The layer of ionized air permits radio waves to reflect back to Earth. The E-layer is 50 to 80 miles upward. The F-layer is 150 to 200 miles up and several layers in between when the E and F layers split. The temperature of the ionosphere ranges from 1,000 degrees Fahrenheit to 1500 degrees Fahrenheit during the day and 300 degrees Fahrenheit at night.

The Exosphere – The furthest atmospheric layer from the Earth is the exosphere. The particles are at the hottest reaching a temperature in excess of 4,500 degrees F. The particles are most fiercely struck by cosmic rays to the point where they only exist as atoms instead of molecules. However, at night, while away from the rays of the sun, the temperature reaches absolute zero, which is -460 F.

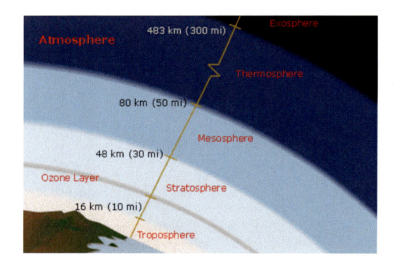

Auroras – The movement of streams of solar particles, 50 to 600 miles up, create the image of an aurora. Auroras are seen mainly at high latitudes and that is because the Earth is a giant magnet and the ionized particles are at their strongest near the poles.

Colors in the Sky – Color is a characteristic of the Earth's atmosphere. At the surface, our sky appears to be blue. Twenty miles from the surface the sky darkens to an almost black. Our sky is blue because the sun's light is scattered in all directions and the short blue wavelengths render a blue hue which is prevalent. Sunsets and sunrises appear to be red simply because the light has more atmosphere to pass through. The color is sometimes enhanced due to the excessive dust in the air. The clouds, haze, and fog appear to be white because all wavelengths are scattered equally.

Other characteristics of a colorful event occur from **Mother-of-Pearl clouds**. This type of elongated cloud occurs between 14 to 19 miles above Earth's surface and consist of water vapor. The bands appear as pastel colors.

The highest clouds know are the **noctilucent** clouds. Comprised of meteor dust, they appear at sunset at a height of 50 miles. The tops of the noctilucent clouds are blueish-white while the edge at the horizon is a gold color. Both mother-of-pearl clouds and noctilucent clouds can travel at speeds of 394 miles per hour.

Meteors – Friction with our atmosphere renders an incandescence appearance in the night sky. The meteors are traveling at 90,000 miles per hour when they hit our atmosphere. The friction rapidly heats up the meteor as it disintegrates to dust 30 miles from the surface of the Earth.

Composition of Dry Air

Component:	Percent of Air
Nitrogen	76.08
Oxygen	20.95
Argon	0.93
Carbon dioxide	0.032
Neon	0.001
Helium	0.0005
Methane	0.00015
Krypton	0.00011
Hydrogen	0.00005
Nitrous oxide	0.00003
Carbon monoxide	0.00001
Ozone	0.00004
Xenon	0.000009
Water	less than 1
Other gas traces	<0.000001

Chapter 3. The Water Cycle - Water in the Atmosphere and Heat

Every day, heat causes millions of tons of water to be evaporated into the atmosphere. Water from the oceans, lakes, and streams experience the vast amount of evaporation, however plant life also generates massive amounts of evaporation. One apple tree can move 1,800 gallons of water to evaporate into the air in a single six month growing season. Water evaporating from leaves is called **transpiration**. Some of the precipitation falls to the ground and replenishes the streams, rivers, and groundwater which in turn provides water to the plant life and the cycle continues to repeat the process. Some of the groundwater becomes trapped creating an underground reservoir called an **aquifer**.

The water in the moist warm air rises and cools. When it reaches 100% relative humidity it condenses and forms a cloud. Depending on the temperature, the condensed clouds will form precipitation and fall as rain or snow. The process of evaporation, condensation, and precipitation is called the **water cycle.** To further expand on the water cycle process it would include evaporation, transpiration, water vapor transport, condensation, precipitation, runoff, and streamflow. This process is also called the **hydrologic cycle**.

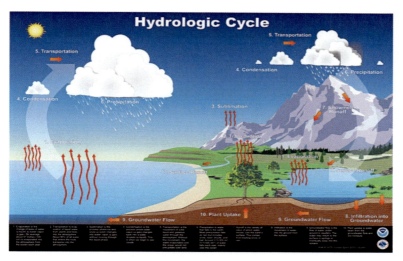

The primary component of the water cycle is precipitation. Precipitation deposits fresh water on Earth. It is estimated that 121,000 cubic miles (505,000 cubic kilometers) of water falls on our planet every year. It is also determined that a portion of that amount, 95,000 cubic miles (398,000 cu km) of precipitation falls over the oceans every year, while 26,000 cubic miles (107,000 cu km) falls over the land. Calculating the surface of Earth would mean that 39 inches (990 mm) of precipitation would fall over Earth each year. In reality, it actually is 28.1 inches (715 mm) of precipitation that falls over the Earth yearly. The Koppen climate classification system uses the average rainfall to determine climate in various regions.

The development of precipitation can include orographic or stratiform rainfall. A strong vertical movement may cause the overturning of the atmosphere in a particular area within an hour. This will cause heavy precipitation. The stratiform (i.e. uplift over a mountain) process is a weaker uplift and will result in less precipitation. Precipitation falls into three categories. It is based on whether the precipitation falls as a liquid or a liquid that freezes on contact with a surface, or as ice. Rain and *drizzle* that freezes on contact with a subfreezing air mass are referred to as *freezing rain*. The frozen forms of precipitation are snow, ice pellets, hail, ice needles, and graupel.

Hydrometeor

The hydrometeor concept is where precipitation, while in the atmosphere, is measured. Solid water or liquid in the atmosphere is referred to as hydrometeors. This includes mist, fog, clouds, haze, and *virga* which is precipitation that evaporates before it touches the ground. Particles from the ground are included as hydrometeor substance even though it had already touched the Earth. This includes sea spray and blowing snow.

Chapter 4. Clouds

Clouds form when water reaches the saturation point and condenses. The water droplets or ice crystals in the air rise and the pressure decreases causing the formation of a cloud. The adiabatic cooling of the air as it rises is about five and a half degrees for every 1,000 feet of altitude. When the pressure drops and the air reach its dew point, the water in the air either condense or forms ice crystals around the small particles in the air such as dust or salt from the oceans. These droplets are a small fraction of the size of a medium sized raindrop. Because they are so small, the turbulent wind in the upper atmosphere maintains the condensed droplets aloft, thus forming the visible cloud. When the cloud is long lasting and thick, it can produce rain droplets or snowflakes heavy enough to reach the ground. Usually, the precipitation is associated with a low-pressure system. When water droplets rise in a high-pressure system, they evaporate.

The types of clouds were named by an English scientist named Luke Howard in 1803. Clouds are classified by shape. Cirrus clouds refer to the tendril of hair. Stratus clouds refer to a spread out like a blanket. Cumulus clouds are referred to a pile or heap. Nimbus clouds are referred to rain. There are ten main types of clouds: cirrus, cirrostratus, altostratus, stratocumulus, cumulus, cirrocumulus, altocumulus, nimbostratus, stratus, and cumulonimbus. These clouds are further classified by their location in the sky or altitude. They are classified as high clouds, middle clouds, low clouds, and towering clouds. Towering clouds may reach an altitude of 75,000 feet.

High Altitude Clouds

It is believed that much of the high altitude clouds are formed by ice or dust from meteorites. These *noctilucent clouds* are very rare because they are very thin and wavy and are seen at night or at dusk as an orange or silver, low density or misty cloud. These clouds are 45 to 54 miles (75 to 90 kilometers) from the surface of the Earth. The base of these clouds is approximately 20,000 feet from the Earth's surface.

Cirrus Clouds (Ci) are the highest clouds forming a thin wispy, feather=like shape and are composed entirely of ice crystals. Their altitude range is between 20,000 to 40,000 feet (6,000 to 12,000 meters). They are sometimes called mares' tails because their shape resembles the tail on a horse.

Cirrostratus Clouds (Cs) are clouds that usually form from 20,000 to 25,000 feet (6,000 + meters). They often cover the entire sky and sometimes form a halo or a luminous circle around the moon or sun. These type of clouds usually indicate that a storm is approaching within 24 hours.

Cirrocumulus Clouds (Cc) These type of clouds are usually in the shape of small white cloud segments. They are icy, patchy clouds in a wave-like pattern. They can be seen from 18,000 to 20,000 feet (5,500 to 6,000 meters). Sometimes they are referred to "mackerel skies" because their shape resembles that of fish scales. Their presences usually indicate that stormy weather is approaching within 24 hours.

Middle Clouds

The stratus or cumulus clouds are generally in the middle cloud area. This area is, on the average, about 10,000 feet but can also appear between 15,000 to 20,000 feet (4,500 to 6,000 meters) above the Earth.

Altostratus Clouds (As) are usually a drab gray, opaque clouds that generally will give the sun and moon a hazy look. They often appear lightly striped. They usually contain water droplets or ice crystals that fall toward the Earth but never reach the surface of the ground. These clouds are the "above" clouds in that they appear in the upper level of the middle clouds, between 15,000 to 20,000 feet (4,500 to 6,000 meters).

Altocumulus Clouds (Ac) This category of middle clouds can be found around 10,000 feet (3,000 meters). These clouds are not made of ice crystals. They are strictly made of water droplets. These clouds appear to be rolls or puffs and are often separated by thin breaks.

Low Clouds

The lowest level of clouds can form near the Earth's surface up to 6,500 feet. There are three types of low clouds in this category.

Stratus Clouds (St) Stratus clouds are wispy in shape and are more like a fog looking type of cloud that hovers a few hundred feet above the ground. They usually form a drizzle type of precipitation and can start as a ground fog. The drizzle occurs because there is a lack of vertical movement of the air.

Stratocumulus Clouds (Sc) These type of clouds are the dark gray clouds that usually cover the entire sky. They normally occupy an altitude of 1,500 to 6,500 feet (450 to 2,000 meters). Often the clear blue sky will break between them. They could be wave-like or rounded. Although these clouds contain water, they do not produce rain.

Nimbostratus Clouds (Ns) These clouds are the low dark rain-bearing clouds. The bottom of these clouds is usually only a few hundred feet above the ground to an altitude of 3,000 feet (900 meters). These clouds produce sleet, snow, and rain, but are not associated with lightning or thunder.

Other Low-Level Clouds:

Cumulus Clouds (Cu) These type of clouds are low-level clouds that develop vertically. They often have dark bottoms with puffy white tops that constantly change. Over land, these clouds form over warm land and disappear at night. They can rise from 2,000 feet to 10,000 feet (600 to 3,000 meters). Generally, they produce a brief shower. The Cumulus clouds are usually a sign of fair weather.

Cumulonimbus Clouds (Cb) These type of clouds are often referred to as thunderheads. They rise up vertically and vary in altitude. Their dark bottoms could be below 5,000 feet (1,500 meters) up to the white anvil-shaped top that can reach up to 50,000 feet (15,250 meters). These clouds contain a large amount of water and often produce hail. The cumulonimbus clouds are either a single cloud in form or a part of a wall of an advancing storm. These violent clouds may produce tornados.

Mammatocumulus Clouds are part of the Thunderstorm type of phenomenon usually on the lower portion of the cumulonimbus cloud.

Chapter 5. Precipitation - Rain, Snow, Ice, Frost, and Dew

Precipitation, according to meteorology, is any form of condensation of the atmospheric water vapor which falls due to the Earth's gravity. The primary forms of precipitation are rain, drizzle, snow, and hail. When a portion of the atmosphere becomes saturated with the water vapor, precipitation occurs. When the water vapor condenses and is not heavy enough to overcome gravity, fog and mist occur. This is not precipitation, it is water vapor suspension. When the air is cooled or more water vapor is introduced to an area, smaller droplets form and remain suspended, thus forming a cloud. When the finer droplets collide and form larger droplets, precipitation occurs. Short periods of rain in various locations are called showers.

A wall of air at a constant temperature, and is not moving with the wind, is called a **stationary front**. When the moisture in the air approaches the stationary front, it is forced to rise upward. As the moist air rises upward, it cools. Condensation of the water vapor can freeze and freezing rain will occur. The condensed water vapor in the rising air will form clouds. The types of clouds are usually stratus or cumulonimbus clouds. When water vapor rises from warmer lakes, lake-effect snowfall may occur which is typically very heavy and concentrated in a geographical area. In mountainous areas, an upslope area will cause the moist air to rise upward, while on the leeward side of the mountain, a dry climate may exist. Because of the terrain, climate occurrences may affect a monsoon zone or rainy seasons. In other climates, a dry or savannah climate may be the dominant weather control.

Precipitation is necessary for life on our planet and is a major component of the water cycle. Precipitation deposits the fresh water on our planet. Approximately 121,000 cubic miles, (505,000 cubic kilometers) of water falls as precipitation each year. Of that amount, 95,000 cubic miles, cu mi) of it over the oceans and 26,000 cubic miles (107,000 cubic kilometers) over land. Given the Earth's surface area, that means the globally averaged annual precipitation is 39 inches, (990 millimeters), however, over land it is only 28.1 inches (715 millimeters).

Rain – When water droplets fuse together to form larger water drop, or when the droplets form a frozen ice crystal, this is called **Coalescence**. Precipitation will only occur when these water droplets coalesce into larger drops. Water droplets collide when air turbulence occurs, thus producing larger droplets. When these droplets become heavy enough to overcome the wind uplift and gravity, the droplets fall to earth as rain. Rain, hail, snow, and sleet will only occur if there are clouds in the sky.

The size of the raindrop can vary from 0.0039 inches (0.1 millimeters) to 0.35 inches (9 millimeters) in diameter. If they fuse to a larger size, the drops will break apart and form new droplets. Very small droplets are called cloud droplets and their shape is that of a sphere. Droplets this small would take 16 hours to fall a half a mile in the still air. These tiny droplets do not fall out of moving air. When raindrops are heavy enough to fall, the bottom portion that is falling against the air is slightly larger than the trailing portion. They are somewhat egged shaped and not the typical teardrop or raindrop image that we commonly see. Raindrops formed from melting hail will typically be larger in size than the normal raindrop.

Rainbows – When the sun comes out shortly after a rainstorm, the light is refracted through the raindrops. Small raindrops refract the most of the light causing the rainbow to be the brightest. The small raindrops at this level are between 1/50 and 1/25 of an inch in diameter. Where the rain is not falling, the rainbow forms more of a partial arc. Sometimes hills or clouds obstruct the sunlight in the blank part of the rainbow. Because of the position of the sun, we can only see the top of the rainbow, otherwise, the rainbow would make a perfect circle. From the ground, we can only see half of the rainbow. From the air, a pilot may see the entire circle of the rainbow.

Ice Prisms – are hexagonal plates, columns, and needles. They glitter in the light as they are blown around. They fall very slowly because of their small size. Ice needles often create halos around the sun or moon. In very cold climates, ice needle will form on the ground.

Diamond Dust – Ice needles, or diamond dust forms at temperatures at -40 degrees F. (-40 C.). This occurs when colder surface-based air mixes with the higher moisture content above. This forms hexagonal shaped ice crystals. When the light is just right, sparkles appear.

Snow – Microscopic bits of sand, soil, clay, or ash often act as the nuclei for water vapor to crystallize which forms snow. The air must be saturated with water vapor and the temperature must be below the freezing point. In the clouds, the temperature would be 10 degrees F. to -4 degrees F. At high altitudes, snow can form without nuclei if the air is saturated with water vapor and the temperature is -38 degrees F. Snowstorms are usually localized storms similar to rainstorms. Snowstorms are a result of vertical air uplift. Cloudy ice particles, usually in the form of needles, columns, or ice plates form the snowflake. As the ice crystals collide, water vapor evaporates causing the ice crystals to grow. Due to their mass, the ice crystals fall through the atmosphere and they stick together as they collide and form clusters. The clusters are snowflakes. The largest recorded snowflake fell in Fort Keogh, Montana in 1887. It was 15 inches in diameter (38 cm). Because of the diffuse reflection of the clear ice crystals, the snowflakes appear to be white. The shape of the snowflake is determined by the humidity and temperature. No two snowflakes are alike and are usually irregular in shape because of the changing humidity, changing temperature, and the time it takes for the snowflake to develop and take shape.

Hail stone

Hail – Hail is precipitation in the shape of lumps or balls and almost form a type of onion shape. Hail is produced in the cumulonimbus clouds (storm clouds). In warm weather, a frozen raindrop forms high in the upper areas of the cloud. As the hailstone gets heavier, it falls through the cloud only to be lifted by the updraft of violent wind currents within the cloud.

As the hail falls and rises repeatedly, it continuously gets super-cooled and additional layers of water droplets form around the surface of the hail. This process can take twenty minutes for the hail to get heavy enough, or the updraft to weaken, to allow the hail to fall to the ground. Hail size can be the size of a pea, 0.2 inch (0.5 cm) to the size of a grapefruit.

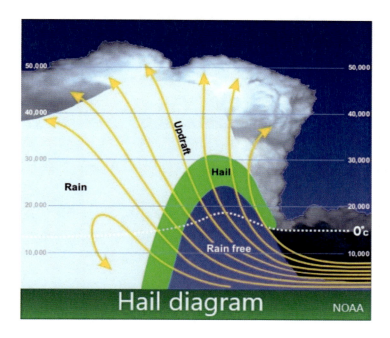

Square Hail

Hail can be destructive

Frozen Water – Water that is frozen comes in many forms.

Frost

Frost – Frost is the result sublimation of the water vapor in the saturated air. This occurs when the temperatures at the surface are below freezing. Frost is similar to a dew, except that it does not condense into water droplets first. Frost forms directly into ice crystals from the water vapor.

Glaze – Glaze is clear and smooth. This coating of ice is hard and dense. This occurs when the super-cooled water attaches to an object that is at a temperature below freezing. Weather producing glaze can be very hazardous in that power line, tree limbs, and poles can be brought down.

Hoarfrost – This 'white' frost is simply ice crystals that form on an object by sublimation. It forms in a similar way as dew, however, the object that it is attached to is below freezing in temperature.

Rime – Rime is white in color and simply a milky deposit of granular ice. Rime is harder than hoarfrost. Rime or snow pellets are soft and do not bounce when they hit the ground.

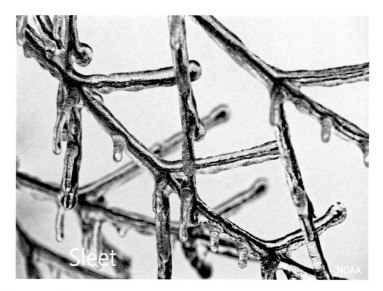

Sleet – Sleet is precipitation in the form of clear or translucent ice pellets. The ice pellets have a diameter of 0.2 inches (5 mm) and easily coats objects with ice on surfaces during an ice storm. Because sleet is hard, it bounces when it hits the ground.

Dew

Dew – Although dew does not fall from the sky, it is, however, water vapor. Solid surfaces that have cooled below the condensation point of the air permits the water vapor in the air to condense and attach to the cold surface. The water droplets that form on the outside of an iced glass is also dew.

Chapter 6. The Motion of the Earth

The Earth does more than simply spin around. The Earth actually has 5 motions. First, the Earth does rotate on its axis every 24 hours. Secondly, the Earth has a slow wobble. Thirdly, it revolves around the sun at 18 ½ miles per second, every 365 ¼ days, which gives us a year. Fourth motion, along with the rest of our solar system, it moves toward the star Vega at 12 miles per second. Lastly, the Earth moves along in rotation with our entire Milky Way Galaxy at 170 miles per second. Two of these motions actually affect weather. The daily rotation of the Earth produces a wind pattern as well as our days and nights. The Earths travel around the sun gives us our seasons.

NOAA

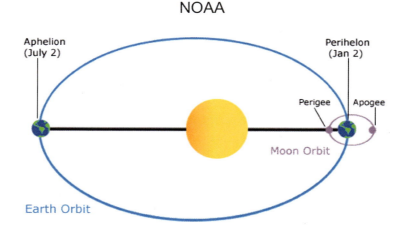

Seasons – The Earth rotates on its axis at 23 ½ degrees of its plane. When the North Pole is tilted toward the sun, the northern hemisphere will have its summer season while the southern hemisphere will have its winter season. When the tilt is toward the sun, the days are longer and nights are shorter. The opposite occurs when the pole is pointed away from the sun. In that occurrence, the nights are longer and the days are shorter.

In the northern hemisphere, the sun is the farthest north on June 22nd. At that time the sun is directly over the Tropic of Cancer and the daylight is at its peak on that day. The North Pole is at its period of six months of daylight while the South Pole is in its period of six months of darkness. During the spring and fall equinox, the sun is equally on both the northern and southern hemisphere. Both day and night are at the equal duration and the beginning of spring or fall season begins.

Summer – There are two primary reasons why summer is the warmer season. The days are longer which gives more exposure to sunlight to warm the Earth's surface. Secondly, the sun's rays are much more concentrated. Most school children know the effect of concentrated sunlight with the use of a magnifying glass. Days and nights are constantly 12 hours long at the equator. The farther north you travel during the summer, the longer the days become. At the North Pole, one would experience the midnight sun. The sun never descends below the horizon. At the same time at the South Pole, the sun never rises above the horizon.

Experiment:

Using an intense flashlight, shine the light at a 27-degree angle on a white piece of paper. With a pen, draw a line around the border of the light image.

Next, shine the light directly on the same piece of paper and draw a line around that light image.

Mark the longer oval as winter and the shorter circle as summer. Note here, that the light concentration is spread over a larger area and is less intense than the light concentration over the 'summer' images.

Activity: Create a chart recording the weather at your location for 30 days.

Daily Weather Log

Date   Observed weather   Temperature   Relative Humidity Wind Direction Pressure   Rain   Forecast

Chapter 7. Measuring and Recording Weather

Basic to accurate weather forecasting depends on collecting data with the use of instruments. Before the instruments were invented, weather prediction was done primarily by folklore. Sailors, farmers, and hunters have always had a need to predict the weather. Some of the folklore predictions were correct much of the time. However, accurate information regarding various factors is required in order to make reliable predictions. Measuring these factors include, air temperature, wind speed, wind direction, air pressure, amount of cloud cover, cloud type, amount of moisture in the air, and the amount of precipitation.

As instruments were invented, such as the thermometer, and the barometer, as well as other instruments, accurate observations and recording methods, induced the creation of the science of meteorology. With worldwide standardizations of time zones based on Greenwich Mean Time and the advent of the telegraph at certain observation points, weather forecasting evolved. Next came the analysis and preparation of weather maps. Currently, worldwide weather maps are created every six hours. Upper atmosphere charts are created every twelve hours. As communication methods have advanced, so have the weather predictions worldwide.

Air Pressure Measurements – To determine the position and movement of weather fronts, a barometer is necessary to plot isobars on a weather map. Air pressure at mountain tops is less than the air pressure at sea level. All pressure readings are calculated and taken as if all readings were at sea level. This permits the accurate mapping of air pressure readings all around the world. There are two types of barometers. The mercurial barometer is used by most weather stations. This type of barometer is closed at the top and filled with mercury to a height of 30 inches. Mercury is a heavy, liquid metal. When reading this type of barometer, when the mercury is high in the tube, there is a high pressure. When the mercury is low in the tube, a low pressure exist. The reading is converted into **millibars**. Millibars are the scientific unit used to measure air pressure. The average height at sea level is 30 inches tall. This type of barometer is precision made and accurate to $1/1000^{th}$ of an inch. A reading of 31 inches would be an indication that the air pressure is very high. A reading below 29 inches would only occur during an extreme cyclone or hurricane.

The aneroid barometer does not contain any fluid. It functions with a corrugated metal container where air has been removed. The container design and the springs included in the instrument prevent the metal container from collapsing. The gears and springs on the dial record the findings. The actual reading of a barometer is not as important as how quickly the change has taken place. A fast change would mean the weather is changing quickly and usually that brings strong winds. A rising high-pressure reading indicates that fair weather is approaching.

An aneroid barometer or barograph contains a paper drum that slowly rotates. The readings are recorded as a line graph and the direction of the pressure, high or low, is detected and recorded.

Temperature Measurements - The air temperature affects humidity and air pressure. The instrument used to measure the temperature is the **thermometer**. There are two types of thermometers: alcohol and mercury. The alcohol thermometer is most commonly used, but each has a specific purpose. Because mercury freezes at -38 degrees F., it is used for temperatures above that gradient. Alcohol thermometers freeze at -179 degrees F. Most weather thermometers have a range of -40 degrees F. to 110 degrees F. In the United States, the unit of measure is in **Fahrenheit,** whereas in the rest of the world, the unit of measure is in metric and is called **Celsius**. The difference occurs at freezing. At 32 degrees F., water freezes. That would be 0 degrees C. and the boiling temperature would be 212 degrees Fahrenheit and 100 degrees, Celsius. The conversion is essentially over the 32 degrees F. range and multiplying 1.8 times each degree.

The **thermograph** is similar to the barograph in that a paper drum records the temperature reading in a line graph format, instead of the barometric readings. The line graph records whether the temperature is raising or lowering over a set period of time.

Wind Sock

Wind Direction – The most common instrument for indicating the wind direction is the **wind vane**. Most wind vanes have an arrow that points in the direction that wind is coming from, <u>not</u> in the direction that the wind is heading. The more advanced wind vane is the *aero vane* which transmits the data in actual time. The sudden shift in wind direction marks the passing of a front.

Wind Speed – The instrument used in measuring wind speed is the **anemometer**. The most common type of anemometer is the cup anemometer which has three or four cups that spin in the wind. Winds speeds are usually measured in miles per hour but can also be measured in meters per second, or knots. A knot is one nautical mile per hour which is about 6,080 feet. A nautical mile is about 15 percent longer than our standard mile which is 5,280 feet. Scientific instruments report measurements in meters per second while aircraft and sea vessels report in knots.

Aviation depends on winds aloft. Often a pilot balloon is used and a theodolite (similar to a surveyor's instrument) measures the angle of the balloon with the ground and its direction. Wind speed and direction are calculated using accurate scales, by the observation made by the meteorologist.

Rain Gauge - The rain gauge used by weather stations usually are in a metallic container. The gauge itself is in the 4 inch (100 mm) plastic variety or the 8 inch (200 mm) standard instrument. The inner cylinder permits 1 inch (25 mm) of rain to enter with the rest overflowing into the outer tube. Calculation markings on a plastic tube will be as low as 0.01 inch (0.25 mm). After the inner cylinder is filled, the amount outside is discarded, and then filled with the remaining precipitation, adding to the overall total until the precipitation in the outer cylinder is empty. In the winter, the inner tube is removed to allow snow and freezing precipitation to accumulate. Meteorologist also add anti-freeze to allow the snow and ice to melt as quickly as possible.

sling psychrometer

Relative Humidity – Humidity is measured with an instrument called a **sling psychrometer**, or a **wet-bulb hygrometer**. The sling psychrometer is essentially two thermometers with one of the thermometers having a wet wick on the bulb. The end is dipped in water before both thermometers are whirled around. The evaporation of the web bulb lowers the temperature of that thermometer. The difference in both thermometers shows the humidity or water vapor in the air. Hygrographs record the humidity. This type of instrument uses human hair. Hair increases in length due to the amount of moisture in the air. The results are recorded as a line graph on a drum. Humidity is important in predicting icing conditions which could cause an aircraft to become unstable.

Precipitation Measurement - All forms of precipitation are measured with a **rain gage**. The accuracy is measured to 1/100th of an inch. Recording the participation is important to farmers in local farming areas may have to plant their crops at different times.

The World's Highest and Lowest Temperatures Recorded-

Temperature	Place	Year
136 F. (58 C.)	El-Azizia, Libya	1922
134 F. (56 C.)	Death Valley, California	1933

Highest Average per Year:

95 F. (35 C.)	Dalol Danakil Depression, Ethiopia	

Recorded Lowest Temperature:

-128.6 F. (-89 C.)	Vostok Station, Antarctica	1983
-79.8 F. (-62 C.)	Prospect Creek, Alaska	1971
-70 F. (-57 C.)	Rogers Pass, Montana	1954

Lowest Average per Year:

-71.7 F. (-56.7 C.)	Plateau Station, Antarctica	

Ceiling Height Measurement – Ceiling height measurement is the altitude from the ground to the base of the clouds. This is particularly important to pilots, especially if the base of the cloud is less than 10,000 feet and clouds cover more than half of the sky. This affects the pilot's visibility to land or take off. The ceiling height is measured in various ways. Aircraft check their altimeter readings. Ceiling balloons are used and measured when the balloon disappears into the clouds. A **clinometer** and a ceiling light projector are used to measure ceiling height at night. The observer stands 1,000 feet from the light projector. The angle is measured and a chart defines the ceiling height. Most airports use a photo-electric cell which rotates vertically at 90 degrees and transmits measurements continuously.

Sunshine Duration Transmitter – This instrument is used to record the amount of sunshine duration each day. This information is important for agriculture, the resort industry, and industry in general. The instrument is a clear, sealed bulb containing mercury. The transmitter has a black bulb containing mercury with a sealed air space above. The black bulb expands when heated pushing the mercury up the tube which makes an electric contact. The signal results in a mark on a rotating graph paper. When clouds cover the sun, the bulb cools. The mercury then shrinks and the electrical contact is broken, hence no signal is transmitted.

Radiosonde Measurement – An electronic device with a radio transmitter is sent aloft via a weather balloon. The purpose of this instrument is to measure temperature, humidity, and pressure in the upper atmosphere. Radiosondes are sent up twice daily by the National Weather Service. Often, these radiosonde instruments reach an altitude of 100,000 feet or more.

Radar Equipment – This is the most common form of weather detection today. Radar is carried on planes and more often fixed to stationary points on the ground. Recently, mobile vehicles, carrying sophisticated equipment have been deployed into storm areas.

Weather Satellites – The first weather satellite was launched on April 1, 1960. The satellite was called TIROS (Television and Infra-Red Observation Satellite). The TIROS satellites were equipped with cameras, radiometers, and other equipment. Because clouds outline weather fronts, the photographs taken were used to determine fronts particularly in areas that observations were not made. The TIROS satellite leveled at an altitude of 400 miles and rotated around the Earth every 100 minutes. Since then, satellites are more advanced technologically. They are now in a continuous watch over the entire Earth. This occurs because the NOAA has two satellite systems in progress. The Polar Operational Environmental Satellites (POES) passes over the poles at an altitude of 520 miles and circle the Earth approximately every 100 minutes. These satellites are in synchronous orbit with the sun so that they can pass over the same spot in orbit every day. These satellites record atmospheric and ground observations.

About 22,300 miles above the equator, the geostationary satellites are positioned. These satellites remain in a stationary position at the same speed of the Earth's rotation. This method is called *geosynchronous*. This satellite system is called the Geostationary Operational Environmental Satellites (GOES). Images are recorded every five minutes and sent back to the central weather stations. The frequent recording allows meteorologist to view cloud motions including areas over oceans where observations are scarce.

Readings from both satellite systems are conducted day and night. Visual equipment is used for daylight views and Infrared equipment is used for night observations. Observations are made of temperature, moisture, clouds, ocean, land, agriculture, and other vegetation. These advanced satellite systems continuously improve the numerical weather forecasting systems.

Satellite Readings

The surface weather instruments are used worldwide and are very accurate. However, large areas of our planet are not positioned to handle continuous accurate readings. The areas such as the oceans and remote areas on mountain ranges and deserts. In some areas, political boundaries prevent meteorologist and their equipment to maintain a presence. For those reasons, modern global observation of the weather is largely dependent on satellite functions. Satellites work remotely and using its onboard sensor equipment, sends information back to weather centers regarding precipitation and the intensity of any storm.

The satellites currently in use measure precipitation by using thermal infrared (IR) which record and transmit a channel in the area of 11-micron wavelengths. The recording also includes information regarding the tops of clouds. The temperatures of the cloud tops are associated with the altitude of the cloud. The higher the cloud top, the colder the temperature. The clouds at higher altitudes have a smoother top than the clouds at lower altitudes. The clouds at lower altitudes tend to be more active. Using various algorithms and mathematical schemes, along with other properties, precipitation can be derived from the calculated results.

Another instrument on board the satellite is a microwave sensor. This equipment detects the part of the electromagnetic spectrum needed to analyze data. The microwave equipment utilizes frequencies from ten gigahertz to a few hundred gigahertz. Channels up to the range of 37 gigahertz provide information on rain and drizzle (hydrometeors) in the lower parts of the clouds. Larger amounts of precipitation emit larger amounts of microwave radiant energy. Snow and ice scatter the microwave signals at that frequency.

Soon newer satellites will be deployed to use additional sensor channels needed to provide information regarding additional IR channels, atmospheric sounding retrievals, water vapor channels, and visible channels.

Chapter 8. High Pressure, Low Pressure

Because of the unequal heating of the Earth between the poles and the equator, the creation of winds is inevitable. Of course, the Earth's rotation is a major factor in the wind creation, but so is the resulting air circulation patterns. This causes whirlwinds that create high-pressure systems and low-pressure systems. The highs, sometimes called *anticyclones*, usually bring fair weather. The low, *cyclones*, usually bring unsettled weather. In regions with the prevailing westerlies, the high cells travel from west to east.

Let's take a look at the high-pressure and low-pressure effects:

	HIGHS	LOWS
Weather:	Generally fair	Brings clouds, rain, or snow weather
Circulation:	Clockwise in the north the northern hemisphere	Counter-clockwise in
	Counter-clockwise southern hemisphere	Clockwise in the
	In the southern hemisphere	
Winds:	Light	Strong, gusting
Temperature: warm in the tropics	Warm or cold for long periods Changing to cold quickly	Very

Where air cools, compresses, and sinks toward a lower altitude, a local high-pressure area will develop. The horse latitudes and the polar latitude in the northern hemisphere are two high-pressure systems. This is because the air builds up, becomes heavy and settles toward Earth. Where these high-pressure regions develop, it slowly moves in a clockwise, spiraling motion, or anticyclone. The high air pressure moves toward the lower air pressure region. Because of the Earth's rotation, it moves toward the right. Air moving toward the south shifts to the west; air moving north, shifts to the east. These high-pressure cells move southward from the polar region.

If you can picture the ocean of air surrounding the Earth as a shell of air with peaks and valleys, you would be quite accurate. Air from a high will flow downhill and because of the Earth's rotation, will spiral as it spreads out toward the low-pressure cell. This occurs more so at the surface and less up in altitude.

High-Pressure Wind Velocities – If you look at a weather map, the isobars look very much like the lines on a contour map. However, instead of showing elevation, the isobars show the variations in air pressure. Where the isobars are close together indicates that the air pressure is changing rapidly and the winds are strong and fast. Where the isobar lines are further apart indicate that the winds are slow. The winds a couple of thousand feet up does not spiral as it does at ground level. This is because the high-pressure cell is affected by the Earth's rotation and not by the friction at ground level. Winds over land spiral about 45 degrees from the source while over the ocean, the spiral is about only ten degrees from the source.

Low-Pressure Formation – When two high-pressure cells are at different temperatures, the waves get larger and break off. This forms a low-pressure cell. Another type of low formation occurs when the air under a large cumulonimbus cloud draws rising air rapidly. The low-pressure is filled by the air rushing inward at a counter-clockwise motion that is due to the Earth's rotation. .These type of cyclones are usually about 20 miles in diameter. Over arid desert regions, a heat low may develop. The hot air expands, rises, and flows outward near the top. At this point, less air piles up, pressure drops and the air surrounding the cell rushes in with a swirling motion. This type of low can last a long time over arid regions.

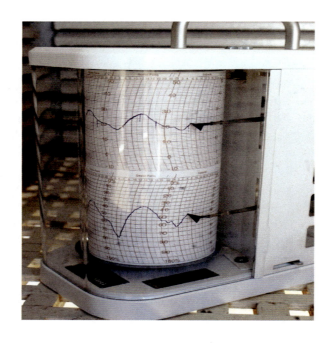

Chapter 9. Wind

Even in prehistoric times, people came to realize that weather, with all of its clouds, cold, warmth, and precipitation, was brought about by the wind with its speed and direction. From as early as the 1600's, it was known that air has weight and it was lighter when the air was warm and heavier when the air was cold. The pressure of the air is determined by its weight.

The Earth's rotation in a key factor in the creation of winds. The Earth is about 25,000 miles around the equator. At the equator, the speed is in the constant movement of about 1,000 miles per hour with the Earth's rotation. Halfway between the equator and the poles, at latitude 45 degrees, the Earth is spinning at 700 miles per hour. At the poles, there isn't any spin speed because of the point where the Earth is spinning on its axis. These variations of speeds impact the effect of winds.

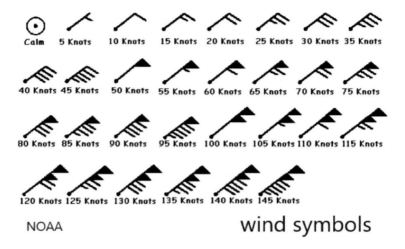

NOAA wind symbols

The Earth's winds are categorized into three groups: planetary winds, secondary winds, and regional winds.

Planetary Winds – The Earth's global winds arise from the temperature belts and the variations in air pressure. Essentially, the warm air heated by the sun at the equator rises and moves toward the poles. The cool air from the poles descend and move toward the equator. As seasons change, the sun's warming of the air changes. The Hadley cell, or tropical cells, rise and fall at the 30-degree latitude. Ferrel cells rise and fall at 60-degree latitude. Because they are rising cells, these cells cause heavy participation between the 40-degree and 60-degree latitudes. On the descending circulation side of these cells an arid condition exists in the subtropics.

The rotation of the Earth affects the **prevailing winds**. This is associated with the **Coriolis Effect**. The variation in pressure at ground level and at higher altitudes create the constant wind direction. The prevailing winds are the polar high, polar easterlies, subpolar lows, westerlies, subtropical high horse latitudes, and trade winds. Along the equator is the equatorial low doldrums.

Secondary Winds – If you've ever been to the beach you would be familiar with land and sea breezes. During warm days, the land is heated by the sun and the higher temperature causes the air to rise. The warm rising air is replaced by the cool air from the ocean or lake. This is often called an *onshore breeze*. The opposite occurs at night. The land cools and the warm water, which retains its heat longer than land, causes the warmer air to rise and the cooler air from the land rushes toward the sea to replace the rising warm air. This is referred to an *offshore breeze*.

Monsoons – Because of the difference in the heating of the oceans and land, the winds are predictable in the Southeast Asian and India regions. The rain summer monsoon seasons and the dry winter monsoon seasons are a consistent weather pattern.

Regional Winds – Generally, regional winds are affected by the topography of the land. Air that is forced up a mountain is cooled adiabatically. The air is cooled and clouds, rain, snow will fall on the windward side of the mountain. As the air climbs over onto the leeward side of the mountain, the heat from this side of the mountain is warm. The ascending winds are called *anabatic*; the descending winds are called *katabatic*.

Examples of regional winds:

In the area of the Balkan Mountains, the **bora** winds descend the coastal mountains along the coast of the Adriatic between the Albanian and Trieste border.

Some winds can attain speeds of 100 miles per hour (161 Km per hour).

The bitterly cold winds and blizzards associated with Siberia and southern Russia is referred to as the **Buran** wind.

The winds that blow off of the Pacific on the eastern slopes of the Rocky Mountains are called the **Chinook** winds. Most of the precipitation is dropped on the western side while dry, cool winds move down the eastern slopes. This wind will warm and melt the snow quickly. A similar wind in the Alps is called *Faehn*.

In Sudan, they experience sandstorms that can be several thousand feet high. This wind is referred to as the **haboob** wind.

Because of the depression in the Gulf of Genoa, the Rhone valley in France experiences a troubling wind called the **mistral** wind. These winds have reached 125 miles per hour (200 Km per hour). The mistral wind causes forest fires in the spring and a killing frost to the agriculture.

Wind circulation along the mid-Atlantic coast brings a **nor'easter** of New England. These storms are usually violent but move quickly down the east Atlantic coast.

California experiences the hot, dry winds call the **Santa Ana** winds. This effect occurs due to the flow of dry air from a high pressure that interacts with mountainous terrain.

The hot interior of the Sahara Desert brings the **sirocco** winds. The sirocco winds are strong, gusty winds that occur in the leading edge of eastward-moving storms.

Southern Russia experiences the **sukhovey** winds which are a hot, dry, dusty wind. The wind blows in a southerly direction for a few days at a time. It has been harmful to crops in the area.

The Aleutian Islands in Alaska experience the **williwaws**. These winds are caused by the topography of the fjords in the area.

Beaufort Wind Scale – In 1806 Admiral Sir Francis Beaufort developed the Beaufort wind scale. It was created to determine winds speed for sailing ships. In 1946, a weather instrument called an anemometer was created and used to measure wind speed.

Force	Miles per Hour	Conditions
0	1	Light wind. Smoke rises vertically
1	1-3	Light wind. Smoke drifts slowly
2	4-7	Light wind. Wind is felt on the face and rustles leaves
3	8-12	Gentle wind. Leaves and small twigs in constant motion
4	13-18	Moderate wind. Dust blows and small branches move
5	19-24	Moderate wind. Small trees sway; small crest on water
6	25-31	Strong wind. Large branches in motion; wires whistle
7	32-38	Strong wind. Whole trees in motion; walking is a burden
8	39-46	Gale wind. Twigs break off trees
9	47-54	Gale wind. Slight structural damage
10	55-63	Strom wind. Smaller trees uprooted

| 11 | 64-74 | Violent wind storm. Widespread damage |
| 12 | >74 | Hurricane winds. |

Wind Chill Chart

Wind (mph) \ Temperature (°F)	Calm	40	35	30	25	20	15	10	5	0	-5	-10	-15	-20	-25	-30	-35	-40	-45
5		36	31	25	19	13	7	1	-5	-11	-16	-22	-28	-34	-40	-46	-52	-57	-63
10		34	27	21	15	9	3	-4	-10	-16	-22	-28	-35	-41	-47	-53	-59	-66	-72
15		32	25	19	13	6	0	-7	-13	-19	-26	-32	-39	-45	-51	-58	-64	-71	-77
20		30	24	17	11	4	-2	-9	-15	-22	-29	-35	-42	-48	-55	-61	-68	-74	-81
25		29	23	16	9	3	-4	-11	-17	-24	-31	-37	-44	-51	-58	-64	-71	-78	-84
30		28	22	15	8	1	-5	-12	-19	-26	-33	-39	-46	-53	-60	-67	-73	-80	-87
35		28	21	14	7	0	-7	-14	-21	-27	-34	-41	-48	-55	-62	-69	-76	-82	-89
40		27	20	13	6	-1	-8	-15	-22	-29	-36	-43	-50	-57	-64	-71	-78	-84	-91
45		26	19	12	5	-2	-9	-16	-23	-30	-37	-44	-51	-58	-65	-72	-79	-86	-93
50		26	19	12	4	-3	-10	-17	-24	-31	-38	-45	-52	-60	-67	-74	-81	-88	-95
55		25	18	11	4	-3	-11	-18	-25	-32	-39	-46	-54	-61	-68	-75	-82	-89	-97
60		25	17	10	3	-4	-11	-19	-26	-33	-40	-48	-55	-62	-69	-76	-84	-91	-98

Frostbite Times: 30 minutes, 10 minutes, 5 minutes

$$\text{Wind Chill (°F)} = 35.74 + 0.6215T - 35.75(V^{0.16}) + 0.4275T(V^{0.16})$$

Where, T= Air Temperature (°F) V= Wind Speed (mph)   Effective 11/01/01

Major Wind and Pressure Systems

Region	Name	Pressure	Surface Winds	Weather
Equator 0˚	Doldrums (ITCZ)	Low	Light	Abundant precipitation, Cloudiness, hurricane Starts. Low salinity.
0˚-30˚	Trade Winds		Northeasterly in N. Southeasterly in S.	Summer wet, winter dry; tropical storms
30˚ less	Horse latitudes	High	Light	Dry all seasons; Cloudiness. High Sea salinity.
30˚-60˚	Prevailing Westerlies	Wet. Subtropical high	-Southwest in N. And low pressure.	Summer dry; Winter
60˚N	Polar front	Low	Variable	Cloudy weather zone, Stormy; all season Precipitation.
60˚-90˚	Polar easterlies		-Northeast in Northern Hemisphere	Cold polar air.

Southeast in Southern Hemisphere   Low temperatures.

90°   Poles   High   Southerly in Northern Hemisphere   Dry, cold air.   Little precipitation.

Chapter 10. Fronts

A weather front is a well-defined boundary between air masses. There are four types of weather fronts, cold, warm, stationary, and occluded. A **cold** front occurs when a cold air mass is followed by a warm air mass. A **warm** front occurs when a warm front is followed by a cold front. A **stationary** front is identified by the fact that the front is not advancing. When cold, warm, and cool air collide, it is referred to as an **occluded** front.

Fronts are associated with bad weather. When a cold air mass moves under a warm air mass, the boundary is stationary. If the warm air front pushes over the cold air mass, it is called a warm front.

Front facts:

(1) The fronts form at the margin of a high-pressure cell.
(2) Only cells with different temperatures form a front.
(3) The warm air always slides up over cold air.
(4) If a front approaches a low-pressure trough, the pressure drops as the front approaches and rises quickly after the front passes by.
(5) Wind near the ground always spirals clockwise in the northern hemisphere, as the front passes.
(6) Wherever the advance of a front, cold air will always slope over the approach or rear of the direction of the front.

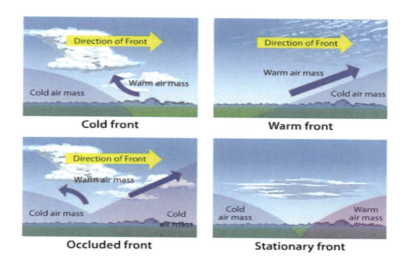

Equatorial and Polar Fronts – Conditions for a permanent front are ideal at latitude 30 degrees. Prevailing westerlies from the southwest run into the polar easterlies from the northwest. The westerlies are warm and the polar air is cold. Polar air builds up the pressure and it breaks through to form the masses of continental polar air or maritime polar air that sails over the North American continent. In the U.S., air from this front impacts the eastern and central states.

The equatorial front is not a true front because the temperatures north and south are about the same. In late summer the temperatures move northward which influences the production of hurricanes.

Winter Fronts – As the continents warm up, air pressure is lowered. Polar fronts move further south. Wind and temperature differences between and land and sea move fronts back and forth. The most active fronts during the winter are the northwestern parts of the Pacific and the northwestern parts of the Atlantic. The fronts east of the Rocky Mountains move southeastward which brings weather changes.

Summer Fronts – Summer fronts are weaker than winter fronts because of the warming of the continents. The fronts do not move as far south as the winter fronts do. Because of the prevailing westerlies, the front is held back from spreading over the southernmost states. The maritime tropical air pushes north and renders very warm weather in the northern hemisphere.

Warm Fronts – The advance of a warm front is usually around 15 miles per hour and that is about half the speed of a cold front. The vertical advance between a warm and cold air mass in a warm front is less steep than in a cold front. Ground friction slowly drags the bottom edge of the retreating cold air mass forming sort of a wedge. Generally, a warm front extends over a massive area of several hundred miles. A cloud sequence might be noticed a thousand miles in advance of the front or 48 hours in advance of an approaching front. Precipitation occurs when the warm front comes into contact with cold air.

When a warm front approaches, it first displays cirrus clouds which have risen farthest up the cold air slope. A check on the barometer shows that the barometric pressure is falling. Then the mackerel sky appears, these are the cirrocumulus clouds. This indicates that the warm air above is unstable. The barometer shows that the presser if still falling. If the warm air overhead is stable, the clouds are replaced by middle high altostratus clouds. The barometer will continue to fall. As the altostratus clouds become dense, precipitation will begin to fall. The dense clouds will remain until the front has passed. If the front is stable, cumulonimbus clouds will mark the end of the passing front.

Stationary Front – If the front remains stationary, the air may be mild but the precipitation can remain for days until one front moves the other.

Weak Front – Usually a weak front will go unnoticed. This occurs when both fronts are the same in humidity and temperature. The only difference is a difference in wind direction.

Warm Air that is Stable – As a warm front approaches it is lifted over a cold front, the formation of stratus clouds appear. The order of cloud format is stratus, nimbostratus, altostratus, cirrostratus, and cirrus clouds. Precipitation is heavy in the beginning, however, as the front is lifted at 20,000 feet or higher, dry cirrus clouds will form and the precipitation will subside.

Warm Air that is Unstable – An unstable air mass produces the most violent weather. The unstable air causes air to rapidly rise creating cumulonimbus clouds and thunderstorms. Precipitation is spotty after a downfall at the beginning of the front. The heavier downpour turns into a gradual drizzle.

Cold Fronts – A cold front will wedge its way under a warm front. In the northern hemisphere, the cold fronts usually flow from the northeast to southwest direction. Cold fronts are almost always head northeast to southwest. A slow moving cold front will generate nimbostratus clouds and thunderstorms.

The Life of a Frontal Low – Fronts in the northern hemisphere tend to move in an easterly or south-easterly direction. Warm fronts are followed by cold fronts. Along the frontal line, the low-pressure cell forms a wave-like shape and bulge out from the frontal line. (1) The frontal line appears at the low-pressure trough, directly between the warm and cold air mass. (2) Cold air pushes under the warm air forming the wave appearance. (3) The cold air continues to push under the warm air to one side and begins to form a low-pressure area. The warm front advances adding to the developing wave. (4) The cold front moves ahead as twice as fast as the warm front. The low-pressure area expands. Warm air is forced over the low and a distinct crest is formed. (5) The cold front overtakes the warm front causing the warm air to rise. (6) Clockwise movement of air is moving near the ground. The low-pressure disappears as the fronts equalize. The barometer drops significantly and usually, the bad weather is the result.

Occluded Fronts – This occurs when the cold front is close to the warm front and overtakes the warm front lifting the warm air mass upward. When the cold front doesn't quickly catch up with the warm front, both warm air and cool air may rise upward. The comma shape occluded front is formed and surrounding air rushes in to equalize the pressure.

Chapter 11. Storms - Thunderstorms, Hurricanes, Blizzards, and Tornadoes

The weather that people fear the most besides a frontal storm are thunderstorms, hurricanes, and tornadoes. To alert the public of these events, the National Weather Service issues watches, warnings, and advisories. A **watch** means that conditions are favorable for a severe weather event. A **warning** means that the severe conditions already exist or are heading the affected direction. A weather **advisory** means that hazardous conditions exist and the public is expected to take precautions.

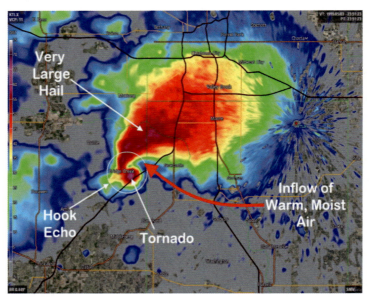

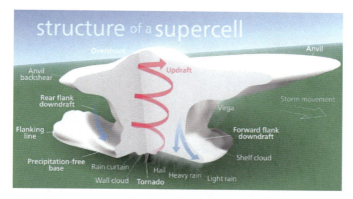

Supercell — NOAA

Rainstorms – A cloudburst is a very heavy downfall of rain which often results in a flash flood since the ground and drainage cannot absorb a large amount of water in a timely manner.

Snowstorms – Intense storms occur in the winter when low pressures systems (cyclones) generate low temperatures, snow, and blustery winds. If the wind is 35 miles per hour or more in a snowstorm, the visibility is less than a quarter of a mile. If these conditions exist for three hours or more it is considered a **blizzard.** An ice storm caused by drizzle falling on frozen objects will cause hazardous conditions. This is especially true if power lines and tree branches fall.

Snowstorms are usually localized storms created due to an updraft of air into the atmosphere. The snow consists of clear and cloudy ice particles which form ice needles, plates, or columns. These particles group together and form the snowflake pattern.

Greatest Annual Snowfalls in the U.S.

Location	Inches	Centimeters
Blue Canyon, CA	240.8	611.6
Marquette, MI	126.0	320.0
Sault St. Marie, MI	116.4	295.7
Caribou, ME	111.5	283.2
Syracuse, NY	110.5	280.7
Mount Shasta, CA	104.9	266.4
Lander, WY	103.9	263.9
Muskegon, MI	98.4	249.9
Sexton Summit, OR	97.8	248.4
Flagstaff, AZ	96.4	244.9

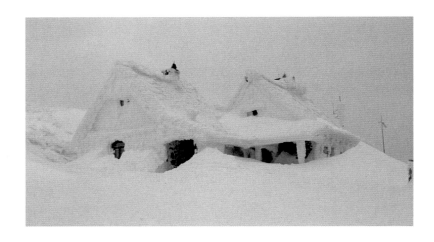

In winter storms, the extreme cold can be very dangerous. Frostbite or hypothermia can mean the loss of life or limb. Hypothermia occurs when the body temperature falls below the normal temperature of 98.6 degrees. If you are caught in this situation without shelter, you should cover your body parts as much as possible and stay dry while trying to contact help. If you are in a vehicle, remain in the vehicle. Make sure that the exhaust pipe is clear as not to back up carbon monoxide fumes into the passenger area.

Having discussed winter hazards, it would be best to also include the other extreme; heat hazards during summer months. Under extreme heat conditions, one could suffer from heat exhaustion, sunstroke, or sunburn. Always be aware of your surroundings: (1) seek shade and preferably seek a cooler area such as an air-conditioned facility; (2) drink plenty of fluids;

water is best; (3) never leave children or pets in a vehicle even if the windows are open; (4) Avoid overexposure with the sun.

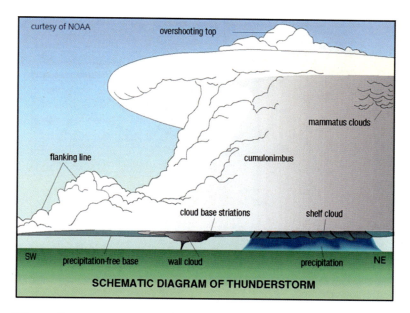

SCHEMATIC DIAGRAM OF THUNDERSTORM

Thunderstorms –Thunderstorms are the result from violent vertical movements of air. The upward draft of air can build up to 75,000 feet. A cause of the uplift of air may be due to the warming of air by the ground, or the temperature difference between land and the ocean. When the air cools to the dew point and a cloud begins to form. Cumulus clouds show updrafts while the cumulonimbus clouds indicate both updrafts and downdrafts. Thunderstorms are localized rainstorms. They are usually accompanied by lightning, thunder, and sometimes hail. Although they can occur any time of the year, they usually occur during the spring and summer months. One developed thunderstorm cell can cover five to ten square miles (8 to 16 kilometers). **Wind shear** or **microburst** occurs when the air below the thunderstorm is dry. The falling rain evaporates in the dry air. The air then cools rapidly and quickly falls down toward the ground.

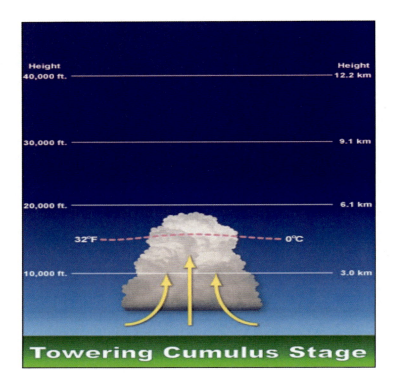

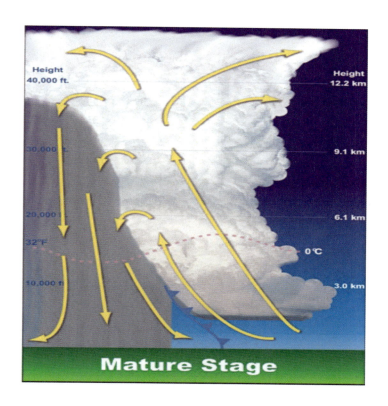

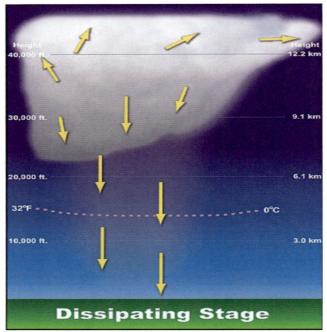

Is the thunderstorm heading toward you or away from you? You will see the flash of lightning before the

102

sound of thunder is heard. Light travels at 186,000 miles per second. Sound travels about 1,100 feet per second through the air. When you see a flash of lightning, immediately count the seconds it takes to hear the thunder. The lightning strike is one mile if you can time five seconds. If the time between the lightning strike and the sound of thunder become shorter in length, then the storm is heading toward you. If the time between the lightning strike and thunder gets longer in length each time you test, then the storm is moving away from you. Thunderstorms generally announce their approach when you note cold air and the downpour of rain approaches. This occurrence can happen three miles before the storm arrives at your location.

Storm Comparisons

Type	Wind Speeds	Width	Duration	Energy
Cyclone	0-50 miles/hour	500-1,000 miles	Week or more	10^{14}
Hurricane	74-200 miles/hour	300-600 miles	Week	10^{15}
Tornado	200-250 miles/hour	1/8 mile	Few minutes	10^{10}
Thunderstorm	20-30 miles/hour	1-2 miles	Hour or less	10^{9}

Lightning and Thunder – In a thunderstorm, lightning is discharged which forms oxides of nitrogen which is water absorbing (hygroscopic). The oxides are added into the air which becomes the nuclei for condensation which induces coalescence, and eventually rainfall.

A lightning bolt and thunder is the result of the explosive release of electrical energy. The rising and falling of air currents create friction which builds up an electrical charge. The electrical charge is transferred through the raindrops, hail, and ice pellets. This charge is about 300,000 volts per foot or 1 million volts per meter. The falling stream of electrons creates a negative charge at the lower part of the cloud. The rising electrons create a positive charge in the upper part of the cloud. The two charges are neutralized in the form of lightning. The Earth is normally a negative charge. Internally, within the cloud, is where the first 65% of discharges occur. In less than one-tenth of a second, a single lightning discharge can strike back and forth. A single lightning discharge can release 30 million volts with 100,000 amperes. The sudden heat from the bolt of lightning rapidly causes air to expand and detract. This compression shockwave is what is known as thunder. Never stand in an open field or under a sole tree, power lines, or wire fences during a thunderstorm. If you feel a tingling sensation on your skin during a storm, find shelter fast. If you can't get to a shelter, squat down on the balls of your feet and cover your ears and place your head between your knees. Never lie flat on the ground since that would make you a larger target. An automobile would be a good place to seek shelter since the rubber tires are an insulation protection. Just avoid touching any metal parts of the car. Also, avoid wading through puddles since downed wires could remain live. Also, avoid touching metal fences.

After a lightning flash, count the seconds it takes for the sound of thunder to reach you. If it takes five seconds for the sound to reach you, the storm is one mile away. It takes five seconds for sound to travel one mile since sound travels at 1,100 feet per second and one mile is 5,280 feet.

Floods – People that live along a river usually experience flooding. The torrential rains from a thunderstorm and cause the banks of the river to overflow and the rushing stream of water can cause severe damage. In some locations, when the spring rains combined with the melting snow, the river basin and streams can quickly overflow. In some locations, **flash floods** quickly destroy everything in its path. If you are caught in a flooded situation, move to higher ground quickly. Do not run or drive into a flooded spot and not know how deep the flooded spot has retained.

Tornadoes – Surprisingly, tornadoes have less energy than most storms, however, the concentration of that energy renders this weather event, the most violent. The dark funnel-shaped cloud from the sky, usually from the bottom of a cumulonimbus cloud, is sometimes called a *twister*. Tornadoes usually travel from the southwest toward the northeast. Their duration on the ground is usually between 5 to 10 minutes. Normally the path of destruction is about 1/8th of a mile wide to 1 mile wide (.2 to 1.6 km) and 100 miles long. Smaller tornadoes sometimes only cause damage when they make contact with the ground. Their winds can reach 300 miles per hour. The fastest tornado recorded was 440 feet (134 meters) per second.

Most tornadoes occur in the United States and Australia during certain seasons. In the U.S. the tornadoes peak during the winter and spring seasons. An average of 124 tornadoes strikes the United States each year. Most strike in the lower Mississippi Valley. On the average, a study of 92 tornadoes, 72 were found to precede a cold front with an average distance of 165 miles. Approximately 25 percent of tornadoes occur between 4 p.m. and 6 p.m., while 80 percent occur between midnight and noon the next day. The air pressure can drop 10 percent in just a few seconds. This drop causes most of the destruction.

Tornadoes develop in four stages. (1) First Mammatocumulus clouds form; (2) the funnel cloud begins to form; (3) the funnel cloud begins its course; (4) the funnel cloud picks up debris and dust. Much of the debris is what causes death and destruction. The debris is traveling hundreds of miles per hour and like shrapnel from a bomb, it tears through anything in its path. Most casualties from a tornado are from the flying debris. If you are in the area of a tornado, don't take shelter near a tree. Trees become the flying debris that is harmful in a tornado. Find shelter in a secure area that will withstand the debris. Find a low spot that will not flood, cover your head and lay flat. Make yourself as small as possible to avoid flying debris. Many people in tornado-prone areas know to take shelter in a storm shelter, basement, and a doorway, bathtub, under a stairway or well-structured workbench. When returning after the storm, be alert to downed power lines and leaking gas mains.

My personal first experience with a tornado occurred while I was stationed at Amarillo Air Force Base, in Amarillo, Texas. It was a dark winter evening and like most airmen on base, we went to the base movie theater. Amarillo is part of the panhandle region which is very flat geographically, and prone to gusting winds. We were all accustomed to the almost daily wind gust. At this time, it was dark, extremely windy and the rain was blowing horizontally. The long line of airmen which stretched a couple of blocks were in a crouching position. We were all almost crawling. We made it back to our barracks and I had barely noticed that there was no one around. I simply assumed that everyone was in there own rooms. I had entered my room and started to write a letter when suddenly my door opened quickly and an airmen yelled "Hey! What are you doing? We're having a tornado. Open the windows and take shelter!" and so I did just that. When I had entered the sheltered area, I had continued writing my letter, "Hey, guess what happened? A tornado!" When I had entered the base, I had noticed that there were no buildings over two stories high. Now I know why. The military procedure for a tornado is to open all of the windows on the second floor and close all of the windows on the first floor. In that particular event, the roof from the NCO club was torn off in the tornado. I was only two streets away from that building but never saw the funnel. Maybe that was a good thing!?

Fujita and Pearson Wind Damage Scale

Tornado Rank	Miles per Hour	Km per hour	Damage
F-0	up to 72	116	Light
F-1	73 – 112	117 - 180	Moderate
F-2	113 – 157	182 – 253	Considerable

F-3	158 – 206	254 – 331	Severe
F-4	207 – 260	333 – 418	Devastating
F-5	261 – 318	420 – 512	Incredible
F-6	319 – 380	513 – 611	not expected

Using air pressure as a means of forecasting the weather. The larger the change in air pressure, the faster the change in weather will occur. When a barometer drops, a low pressure is approaching and rain is likely. When the barometer shows a rise, this would indicate that a high pressure is approaching and fair weather is expected.

Tornado layers
NOAA

Tornado ready to touch ground

Dust Devil — NOAA

Hurricanes – form over tropical ocean areas, in late summer in the area of 5 degrees and 20 degrees northern latitude. The sun heats up large areas of moist air. The moist air rises in a spiral motion. As the air rises up the column, it gains energy and strength. The clouds and wind form a low-pressure called an *eye*. The eye will be 20 to 30 miles in diameter (32 to 48 km). The eye will have an air pressure 6 to 7 percent lower than the remaining system. Most storms die out before they become a hurricane. A hurricane starts as a low-pressure tropical storm. The tropical depression becomes a hurricane when it sustains winds at 74 miles per hour (119 km). Within the eye, low clouds may be present. The moisture within the eye starts to condense and an eyewall is visible. Spiral bands, which are thunderstorms, form and connect to the eyewall in a spiral formation. Wind speeds build up to 150 miles per hour and the entire storm may encompass 400 miles to 600 miles in diameter. Because the temperatures within the system are uniform, the entire weather system moves slowly.

The hurricane begins from the hot moist air mass over the sea. The cyclonic motion starts when opposing trade winds whirl around each other. This occurs when the convergence zone is displaced from the equator. The Earth's rotation contributes to the twisting effect. The rotating low pushes toward the center, forcing hot, moist air upward. The upward motion of the moist air causes rapid condensation. Heat emitted off as the moisture condenses and further warms the rotating air, which becomes lighter and rises faster. More moist tropical sea air rises to replace the updraft. The air inside the storm rises faster and faster.

The difference between a hurricane and a subtropical cyclone is the calm eye found in the hurricane. As the hurricane develops over the seas, it quickly loses energy when it travels over land. When the hurricane approaches land, a storm surge occurs. When the storm surge combines with the normal tide, extensive flooding can be expected. In a hurricane, most deaths that occur are from drowning.

Hurricane sources – In the southwestern part of the North Pacific, hurricanes are referred to as **typhoons**. In this spot, more hurricanes form from there than any other place on Earth. They form between the Marshall Islands and the Philippines and move clockwise toward China, then north toward the Philippines, Korea, and Japan. The second place where hurricanes form frequently is at the South Indian Ocean. Hurricanes in this area are referred to as **Willy-Willies**. These hurricanes form north of Australia and curve northwesterly toward Africa. The third frequency of hurricanes is in the West Indies. The hurricanes from this area usually hit Central America, Mexico, and the southern part of the United States. Of the eight regions that produce hurricanes, only two produce hurricanes that strike the United States. They are the regions of the Mexican West coast and the West Indies. Hurricanes often form where contrasting winds meet. The area is called the

intertropical convergence zone (ITCZ). Hurricanes cannot form at the equator because cyclones require twisting forces. The ITCZ moves north of the equator. The winds are twisted to the right and this causes the cyclonic swirl. In the winter, when the ITCZ moves south of the equator, formations of hurricanes can form in the Indian Ocean and the South Pacific.

Total ATLANTIC HURRICANES BY MONTH OVER 58 YEARS:

Month	Count	Month	Count
Jan	1	Jul	15
Feb	0	Aug	64
Mar	1	Sep	104
Apr	0	Oct	48
May	1	Nov	12
Jun	14	Dec	1

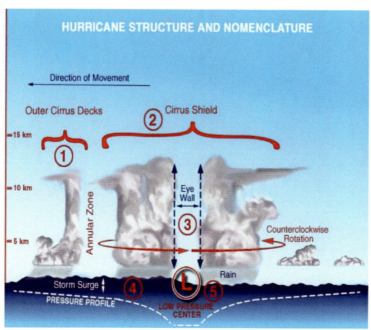

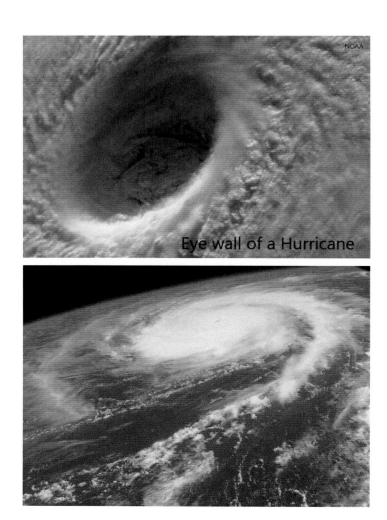
Eye wall of a Hurricane

Chapter 12. Forecasting the Weather

How does the weather affect you? Weather forecasting is defined as the application of technology and science to predict the state of the atmosphere for a future time at a selected location. It affects what you wear when to plant a garden, mow the lawn, turn off the air conditioner and turn up the heat. Weather affects people in different ways, however, weather does affect all of us. To a farmer, the weather helps determine when to plant, fertilize, and harvest his crops. To some livestock farmers, weather determines when to care for his animals. To a commodity investor, the weather would affect prices. To construction workers, who are often paid by the day, need to know when to lay cement, paint, build, and other tasks that would be affected by wind or precipitation, humidity, cold temperatures, hot temperatures and other issues affecting the completion and safety of their job. For sailors and ships at sea are affected by the wind and the condition of the seas. Accurate weather forecast help seaman avoid storms by selecting alternate routes. Aircraft and passengers are affected by the weather regarding delays and cancellations of flights due to bad weather. The safety of the crew during takeoffs and landings is crucial. Ice on the wings and downdrafts can be deadly. Pilots can use the wind to adjust their altitude and speed with a good tailwind. This will allow them to save on fuel cost.

Basically, weather forecasting is applying the science and using technology to predict the condition of the atmosphere for a time in the future for a particular location. Weather forecasts have been made by recording data about the current state of the atmosphere and applying the scientific understanding of the atmospheric process to predict how the atmosphere will change. Before modern technology, humans basically observed changes in barometric pressure, sky condition, and weather conditions at the current state to arrive at the future forecast. Even with modern technology, humans are still required to select the best model to use to arrive at the most accurate prediction. A meteorologist must rely on the pattern recognition skills, model biases, model performance, teleconnections, and be able to solve the equations regarding the massive computational power of the chaotic nature of the atmosphere. The use of model consensus and ensembles help reduce errors and allows the meteorologist make the best predictions.

Predicting Weather by Observation – You probably know more about predicting the weather than you realize. Let's take a look:

1. The wind is blowing gently from the west or northwest. The barometers rise or remain steady. Cumulus clouds appear in the summer sky in the afternoon. What is the prediction?

Prediction - Fair-weather and it will remain fair weather.

2. The wind is blowing from or shifts to the northwest. The night sky is clear and the wind is light. It is winter and the barometer is rising steadily. What is the prediction?

Prediction - The temperature will fall.

3. The sky is clear during the day and cloudy at night. The wind is blowing from the south. What is the prediction?

Prediction -The temperature will probably rise.

4. The barometer is rising rapidly. The east wind shifts to the west wind. Cloud bases start to rise upward. What is the prediction?

Prediction - The weather is clearing.

5. The barometer is dropping. Cirrus clouds are thick and lower level clouds are moving in. Cumulus clouds start to vertically develop. A ring around the moon is noticeable. Winds from the south increase as the clouds start moving from the west. The western sky starts to darken. What is the prediction?

Prediction - Precipitation is on the way.

Using a Barometer and Wind Direction to Predict Weather

– You don't need expensive electronic equipment to predict the weather. An inexpensive aneroid barometer and wind vane will do wonders in predicting your local weather. Follow this chart.

Wind Direction	Barometer	Forecast
SW to NW	30.10 to 30.20 steady	Fair-weather. Steady temperature.
SW to NW	30.10 to 30.20 rising	Fair and warmer temperatures. Rain within 2 days.
SW to NW	30.20 or above - steady	Temperature remains the same. Fair weather.
SW to NW	30.20 or above – falling	Slowly rising temperature. Fair weather for 2 days.
S to SE	30.10 to 30.20 – falling	Rain within 24 hours.
S to SE	30.10 to 30.20 – falling	Wind will increase. Rain within 12 to 24 hours.

Wind	Barometer	Forecast
SE to NE	30.10 to 30.20 – falling	Wind will increase. Rain within 12 to 18 hours.
SE to NE	30.10 to 30.20 – falling	Wind will increase. Rain within 12 hours.
SE to NE	30.00 or below – falling slow	Rain continues one or more days.
SE to NE	30.00 or below – falling fast	Rain and high winds in a few hours. Colder in winter. Clearing in about 36 hours.
E to NE	30.10 or above – falling slow	Summer-with light winds. Rain in 2 to 4 days. Winter- precipitation within 24 hours.
E to NE	30.10 or above – falling fast	Summer-rain in 12 to 24 hours. Winter- Precipitation within 12 hours.
S to SW	30.00 or below – rising slow	Clearing within a few hours. Fair weather for several days.
S to E	29.80 or below – rising slow	Severe storms within a few hours. Then clearing within 24 hours. Cold in the winter.
E to N	29.80 or below – falling fast	Severe storms or heavy gale winds in a few hours. Heavy rain or snow. Cold wave to follow.
To the W	29.80 or below – rising fast	End of a storm. Clearing with cold air coming.

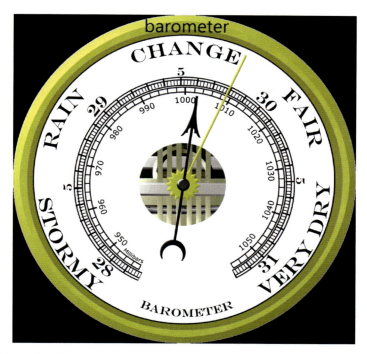

Use of a Barometer –

The barometer has been in use since the 19th century. Forecasting the weather using the measurements over a period of time permitted the early meteorologist a tool to use in forecasting and recording the weather. They've noticed that the faster the change in air pressure had occurred, the faster the change in the weather occurred. Farmers especially needed this information to maintain their crops. If the pressure was of a 'low' pressure drop, they knew that rain is on the way. They also knew that if the 'high' pressure rise occurred, that fair weather conditions were approaching.

Weather and its effect on humans

Since the beginning of time, the weather has had a key effect on people in many different ways. Weather determines our outdoor activities, such as a holiday at the beach in the summer or skiing in the winter. We experience weather through our human senses. We all want to understand weather, how does it change, and how quickly can I find out the future weather.

The weather has influenced historical events in human history. Populations have migrated to different parts on this planet because of the effects of weather. Land bridges permitted mass migration to entire continents. When the polar caps began to melt and the oceans rose, the land bridges became covered with the sea. Entire populations migrated because of desertification. Crops failed and people starved. In the 1690's, famine struck France due to a continued ice climate. In 1696-97, Finland endured severe famine which caused the Finns to lose a third of their population. Historically, the weather has changed the outcome of certain events. For instance, in 1281 the Kamikaze winds prevented Kublai Khan and the Mongol fleet from invading Japan. In 1565, France lost Florida to Spain when a hurricane destroyed the French fleet. Spain captured Fort Caroline and laid claim to Florida. Recently, hurricane Katrina claimed many lives and forced more than a million people to migrate elsewhere when the hurricane struck the United States.

Can Humans Control the Weather?

In some ways, they can and in some ways, they have affected the weather. Humans have always tried to influence the weather. In primitive times people would perform a rain dance to provide water to their crops. Recently, cloud seeding has been employed to cause clouds to condense and create precipitation in order to water the crops. Aircraft equipped with instruments containing silver iodide would spray the tops of clouds. Precipitation would occur and the area intended for precipitation would enjoy the results. Airports benefit from cloud seeding in that fog and low stratus clouds (low ceiling) is lessened. Ski resorts benefit from cloud seeding where clouds over mountains condense and the precipitation falls as snow.

On August 8th, 2008, during the 2008 Summer Olympic Games in China, the government-run Municipal Meteorological Bureau shot 1,104 dispersal rockets into the sky to prevent rain from interfering with the opening ceremonies. The action was recorded as successful in that only 25 millimeters of rain fell whereas the nearby province experienced 100 millimeters of rain on that day.

There have also been unintentional effects on the weather caused by human activity. Agriculture and industry inadvertently caused harmful effects on our planet.

1. Nitrogen oxides and sulfur dioxide put into the air by industry have caused acid rain. This severely has an effect on vegetation, freshwater lakes, and buildings.
2. Air quality and visibility have been reduced because of anthropogenic pollution emitted into the atmosphere.
3. Drought, high temperatures, severe storms, and flooding are expected because of human intervention which will cause a climate change.
4. Large metropolitan areas generate a large amount of heat which will affect nearby areas. Just as lake-effect snow occurs in certain regions, so does heat affect neighboring regions hundreds of miles away from the metropolitan area.

Forecasting

Generally, meteorologist relies on records of previous conditions to accurately predict tomorrow's future weather. Simply looking up at the sky will help predict the coming weather pattern. For instance, high altitude cirrus clouds indicate that rainy weather will probably occur within 24 hours or so.

Over mountains, thick cloud cover could be an expectation of coming rain.

Thin cirrostratus clouds high in the night sky may generate halos around the moon. This would indicate an oncoming warm front with rain.

Since clouds or wind prevent the formation of fog, seeing a morning fog event would indicate fair weather is approaching.

When a thunderstorm arrives, that would indicate an approaching cold front.

Clear skies indicate that fair weather is close by.

A straight-line cloud could indicate a tropical cyclone is attached to it.

Meteorologist

Meteorologists are scientists that study weather. Meteorologists usually work for a government agency, research services, industry, radio and television studios, utility companies, or teachers in the education field. There are approximately 10,000 meteorologists employed in the United States. Radio and television meteorologist are either professional meteorologist or reporters.

Basically, the job of the meteorologist is to research the weather, make a scientific conclusion, and disseminate the information as feasibly possible. Now-casting is the ability to forecast the weather within six hours. Usually, showers and thunderstorms can be accurately predicted. With the up to date radar findings, satellite, and observations, an accurate forecast can be made for an additional few hours. Currently, the use electronic systems that accurately use the data and mesoscale numerical model in order to make an accurate forecast. Because the system is so automated, the human intervention is confined to choosing a model based on a variety of parameters, model biases, and performances. Agreement with other meteorologist teams will reduce forecast errors. Humans are still required to analyze model data into the weather forecasts which are presented to the recipient of the forecast in an understandable format.

Analog technique – The complex way of making a forecast is to memorize a previous weather event and make a prediction based on the previous similar weather event. The problem is with the analog technique, is that rarely is any event perfectly similar. This type of prediction is referred to a pattern recognition. Another technique is called teleconnections. Using other systems to pinpoint to locate another system within the general area.

Types of Meteorology

Hydrometeorology

The branch of meteorology that deals with the hydrologic cycle is called *hydrometeorology*. It is the study of the rainfall statistics of storms and its water budget. The hydro-meteorologist prepares forecasts regarding the amount of precipitation whether it is rain, snow, and the prospect of flash flooding. The hydro-meteorologist is also versed in the study of mesoscale and synoptic meteorology, climatology, and a number of other geosciences.

The tools used in weather forecasting are used differently in various fields of meteorology. This can become challenging for the hydro-meteorologist. Different hardware and software systems use different data formats.

Nuclear meteorology

The study of the distribution of gases and radioactive aerosols in the atmosphere is called *nuclear meteorology*.

Environmental meteorology

How industrial pollution dispersion is physically and chemically impacted by the weather based on various temperatures, winds, humidity, and other weather conditions is called *environmental meteorology*.

Renewable energy and meteorology

The mapping of wind power and solar radiation as a source of energy is a new field of meteorology. Renewable energy is a concern for many countries.

Numerical Weather Prediction

In his paper entitled *Weather Forecasting as a Problem in Mechanics and Physics*, scientist Vilhelm Bjerknes in 1904 stated that it could be possible to predict weather from calculations based on natural laws. Understanding atmospheric physics led to the modern numerical weather prediction years later. Lewis Fry Richardson published Weather Prediction by Numerical Process in 1922. He described how small terms in the prognostic fluid dynamics equations that control atmospheric flow could be neglected. He further stated that a numerical calculation scheme could be devised to allow predictions. Richardson's solution pictured a large auditorium with thousands of people working on many calculations. Of course, a large number of calculations needed to solve was too large to feasibly achieve. It wasn't until the use of computers came into being that this feat was accomplished. At first, unrealistic results were attained. It wasn't until numerical analysis discovered that result was due to numerical instability.

Later, in the 1950's, numerical forecasts using computers became realistic. The first weather forecast used this way was *barotropic* or single-vertical-level models. The prediction of large-scale movement of midlatitude Rossby waves, which is the pattern of highs and lows in the atmosphere, was accomplished in 1959.

The chaos theory discovered by Edward Lorenz in the 1960's observed that the chaotic nature of the atmosphere could be viewed mathematically. From this, *ensemble forecasting* was derived. This process is used to determine possible effects of human emissions of greenhouse gases.

Meteorology on a global scale is the study of weather in regard to heat transfer from the tropics to the poles.

Large-scale oscillations use time periods of months such as the Madden-Julian oscillation, or years as with the El Nino-Southern Oscillation. The time periods brings the results into the range of climate with even longer time periods. Numerical Weather Prediction targets air and sea interaction, atmospheric predictability, tropical meteorology, and tropospheric/stratospheric methods.

Today's Weather Tools

Technology continues to advance, particularly in the area of meteorology. Today's meteorologist is armed with Doppler radar, which is so accurate, the meteorologist can predict weather events to the nearest area with great precision.

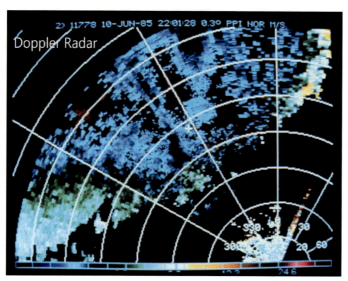

Forecast Communication

Disseminating forecast information is of the utmost importance. Strong winds, lightning, thunderstorms, hail, flash floods can cause deaths or power outages. Drought or frost can destroy crops. Snow and ice can cripple industry and transportation. In order to protect life and property, meteorologist provides weather forecast to the public through watches, warnings, and alerts. Severe weather information is disseminated almost immediately through television, cell phones, radio, and the internet.

Weather Alerts and Advisories

In case of severe or hazardous weather conditions, the national weather service will issue warnings and alerts. A warning or advisory alerts the public that potentially severe weather is near or imminent. A severe weather watch indicates that the danger is more than eminent. The danger has been observed and is within the broadcast area. Listeners would be urged to take shelter immediately or seek higher ground if flash flooding is expected.

How are the Low Temperatures Calculated?

The forecast for the low temperatures for the current day is arrived by using the lowest temperature between 7 pm through 7 am the next day. Today's low temperature will be forecast as tomorrow's low temperature for the day.

Ash Cloud over Valcano

Forecasting Air Traffic

The air industry is most interested in the weather forecast. Low ceilings and for may prevent an aircraft from taking off or landing. Pilots are particularly concerned about icing and turbulence which would affect their in-flight performance. Flights are also very concerned about lightning, updrafts, downdrafts, hail, strong winds, crosswinds, and a microburst. There are many volcanoes on Earth which can erupt at any time. The ash from a volcano can severely damage aircraft engines. Wind direction is important to a pilot because it is beneficial to head directly into a headwind for better lift. This reduces takeoff distance. Pilots also like to take advantage of the jet stream as a tailwind to save aircraft fuel. Aviation meteorology is the concern that weather has on air traffic control. The Aeronautical Information Manual states: *"The effects of ice on aircraft are cumulative—thrust is reduced, drag increases, lift lessens, and weight increases. The results are an increase in stall speed and a deterioration of aircraft performance. In extreme cases, 2 to 3 inches of ice can form on the leading edge of the airfoil in less than 5 minutes. It takes but 1/2 inch of ice to reduce the lifting power of some aircraft by 50 percent and increases the frictional drag by an equal percentage….."*

Pollution Cloud

The aviation industry is alerted when industry creates a cloud within the atmosphere. In this case, the cloud is created from two cooling towers at a nuclear power plant.

Marine Weather Forecasting

All marine vessels are concerned with wind speed, wind direction, wave heights and periodicity, tides, and precipitation. Any miscalculation may cause the vessel to take on water. Recreational and commercial use vessels use the weather forecast to plot a course or schedule their transit. A commercial vessel may lose its cargo or its catch in severe weather. Recreational vessels may lose control of its course in severe weather. The marine weather forecast is communicated over radio via established codes alerting the vessels of the weather and sea condition. The radio used for this forecast are MAFOR, RTTY, Navtex, and Radiofax.

Cumulus Clouds Over Field

Agriculture Industry Forecasting

Farmers depend on the weather forecast to determine which task will be completed that day and to schedule which worker to perform such task. The citrus industry needs to be alerted to a potential frost or freeze weather condition which would destroy the farmers' crops. A drought can destroy corn crops, cotton, wheat, and many other types of vegetation. Together, meteorologist, agronomists, and agricultural hydrologist are involved with the effects of weather on plant distribution, water-use efficiency, crop yield, and the energy balance of natural ecosystems as well as the interaction of vegetation on the weather and climate.

Wildfires

The forestry industry is very concerned about wind direction and precipitation. Forecasting the weather will help determine vulnerable areas that can be subjected to wildfires from human cause or natural causes such as lightning. Harmful insects in a particular are under certain conditions may inflict damage to trees in a particular location.

The Utilities Companies

In order to avoid brownouts or blackouts, the utility companies depend on an accurate forecast to prepare for any anticipated disruption in normal service. On degree day alerts, the utility companies may adjust their power output to meet the consumers' demand. The cooler temperatures force a demand for heating. The warm temperatures place a demand on the power companies at certain times. When people return home from work on a hot day and turn up their air conditioner. At this point, a spike in the power output makes it necessary to adjust for the need.

Chapter 13. Climate

The weather over a certain time (usually 30 years or more) within a particular area is called **climate**. It is a record of weather pattern, including extremes within a certain geographical region. The climate in a particular area will be influenced by its physical conditions which include latitude, ocean currents, prevailing winds, mountains, valleys, and nearness to the bodies of water. Climate is greatly influenced by rainfall and temperature. Of course, the angle at which the sun strikes the Earth in this region affects the climate. As a matter of fact, climate derives from the Greek word *"Klima"* which means angle. The equator receives the sun's direct rays so the climate is generally the same. The poles have seasons and the areas between the poles and equator are called the *temperate zone*. As you may know, the Earth is tilted on its axis. It is about 23.5 degrees on an angle from the plane of its orbit. This gives us our seasons.

Since 1899, the National Weather Service has been collecting data on weather and climate. The data is usually printed on maps for quick and easy analysis. Usually, separate maps are printed for temperature, precipitation, humidity, frosts, storms, sunshine and other climatic data. This important data is used in a variety of ways. For instance, in agriculture, farmers need to know when to plant their crops. Retailers need to know when to put out sales products relating to warm or cold weather. Construction companies need to know when the best times to incorporate particular projects. Personal use of data includes when to plant a garden or paint a house. Many decisions are made using climate charts.

Local climates may be created apart from the general climate of the region. Inland lakes affect local climates. Plants also affect a local climate due to the fact that they absorb a large amount of water. These local climatic differences are called *microclimates*. Farmers sometimes create windbreaks on farms to avoid topsoil from being blown away. This affects the wind currents of the area. Cold air flows downhill thus causing pockets of cold air in the valleys. This is why grapes, oranges, and apples are usually planted on the side of a hill so that there is plenty of drainages when frost occurs. There is also a difference between the country and the city. Heat from the cities creates convection currents. This causes clouds to ascend higher. With a large drainage system in a city, there is less evaporation resulting in less humidity in the city.

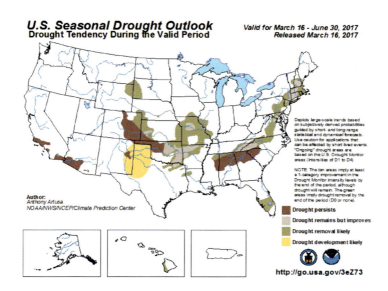

Microclimatic Differences

Forest	Open Land
Wind speeds reduced are higher	Wind speeds
Warmer winter summers	Warm
Water storage is high is lower	Water storage
Relative humidity is higher humidity is lower	Relative

City	Country
Temperature is higher lower	Temperature is
Haze and smog	Clear weather
Less wind speed and radiation speed and radiation	High wind

Valleys vs. Hills

Climatic condition	Period	Valleys	Hills
Minimum temperature	Daily	much lower	higher
Frost	night	more frost	less frost
Fog	morning	more fog	less fog
Temperature range	daily/annual	larger	smaller
Wind speed	night	lower	higher

Climate Change – The Earth is changing all of the time. We've had four ice-ages. The last ice age was from 30,000 to 40,000 years ago. Only sixty-two miles below the surface of the Earth is hot, molten rock and metals. We are barely living on the crust of this large planet that we call Earth. Geological changes have always taken place and will always continue to change. At one point the Earth was so warm that the subtropical weather reached 60 degrees latitude. Polar ice did not exist. Viking ships between 1000 and 1200 A.D. sailed to Greenland easily, however, around 1400 A.D., the route became covered with ice floes and could no longer be traveled in Viking ships.

How much warming will cause a catastrophic effect? What do scientists say that if the average global climate? How is the climate affected by the actions of humans? The natural effects on climate are caused by warming and cooling cycles and wet and dry periods. The Earth's climate naturally changes due to plant life, ocean temperatures, the sun, ocean circulations, natural changes in the atmosphere, and natural changes to the landscape. Weather shapes the Earth. The process of breaking down the soils and rocks into smaller parts is weathering. During precipitation, the rain absorbs and dissolves carbon dioxide from the air. The water becomes slightly acidic which helps in the erosive process. Salt is a combination of a *base* and its opposite, *acid*. The salty, moist air aids the chemical changes that affect the Earth. Other components added to the air causes acid rain. However human intervention has caused climate change in a variety of ways. Areas that were once fertile are now deserts. Some places suffer from overgrazing and unconventional farming methods. Strip mining has damaged the land in many places causing the desertification of the land. The fertile topsoil is stripped or washed away. With the loss of plant life, the soil becomes parched, lacking water. Sand dunes form and recovery is less likely. The dust bowl in the United States brought the attention of better farming control. However, the stripping of the rainforest in South America will eventually have a global impact on our Earth.

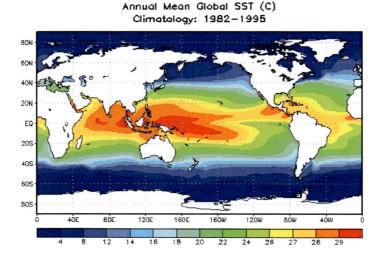
Annual Mean Global SST (C)
Climatology: 1982-1995

Acid Rain – There are a number of pollutants in our atmosphere. Many countries are trying to regulate the number of pollutants that factories, power plants, and vehicles can put into our atmosphere. What goes up, must come down, and usually in the form of rain. The polluted acid rain falls to Earth resulting in damage to forest, crops, the water cycle, outdoor structures, and buildings.

Global Warming – The concern with greenhouse gases is that the layer of gases will eventually envelop the Earth. This envelope of greenhouse gasses would permit the sun's rays from entering the Earth's atmosphere, however, the greenhouse gases would prevent the sun's radiation from escaping back into space. This would cause the Earth temperature to rise which would cause the polar caps to melt. If the polar caps melt that would certainly affect the climate.

Ocean levels will rise, islands and coastlines will flood.

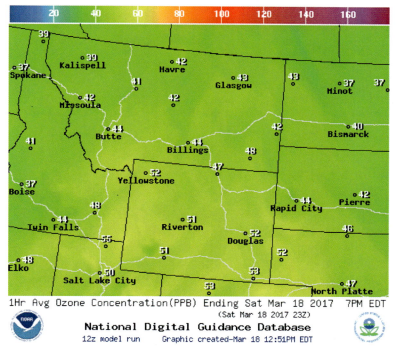

Ozone Layer – The ozone layer is another concern that may affect the climate. Ozone is a three atom oxygen molecule (O3).The oxygen that we breathe is O2. A monoxide is O. Ozone and a monoxide are both poisonous to humans. The ozone layer that we are discussing is about 12 to 15 miles above sea level and located in the stratosphere. It is a very thin layer of ozone gas, approximately only three inches thick. It is very important to life in that it protects us from the sun's harmful ultraviolet rays. Damage to the ozone layer may be due to the use of refrigerants, and solvents used in industry. It is believed that the chlorofluorocarbons (CFCs) are the cause of the breakdown of the ozone layer. Governments around the world are slowly trying to regulate the use of CFCs.

Modern Climate Changes - Evaporation increases when the temperature rises. This leads to more precipitation. The precipitation has increased over land north of latitude 30 degrees from 1900 to 2005. However, precipitation has declined over the tropics from the 1970's to the current date. Nevertheless, statistically, the difference in precipitation has not changed in the past century globally. The eastern parts of the North and South American continents, as well as northern Europe and northern and central Asia, have recorded more precipitation. Parts of southern Asia and Africa have become drier. Over the continental United States, the total annual precipitation has increased by 6.1 percent. Hawaii has had a decrease in precipitation of 9.25 percent. The oceans have shown a decreased amount of salinity in the lower latitudes which have changed the precipitation and evaporation at the mid to high latitude regions. This is a factor for increased precipitation in these areas.

Köppen climate classification –

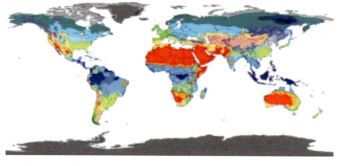

Koppen-Geiger Climate map

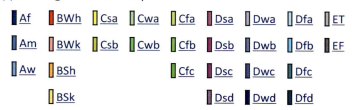

The Köppen classification map relies on the average monthly values of precipitation and temperature. You'll note the five classifications: **A** is tropical; **B** is dry; **C** is the mild middle latitude; **D** is the cold mid-latitude; **E** is the polar region.

Additional classifications include: rain forest, tropical savanna, monsoon, humid continental region, humid subtropical region, steppe area, Mediterranean climate, tundra, subarctic climate, polar ice cap, and desert.

> A rainforest is defined as having high rainfall between 69 and 79 inches (1,750 and 2,000mm) annually.
>
> The tropical savanna is a grassland biome is located in the semi-arid to semi-humid climate regions. Located in the subtropical and tropical

latitudes, the rainfall is between 30 and 50 inches (750 and 1,270mm) annually. These areas are located in the northern parts of South America, Africa, Malaysia, and Australia. The humid subtropical climate regions have a winter rainfall associated with violent storms. Most humid subtropical climates are located on the east side of continents, between the 20 degree and 40-degree latitudes. The humid subtropical climates lie on the east side of continents, between 20 degrees and 40 degrees latitude.

Maritime climate, or oceanic climate, is located along the west coasts of continents, at the middle latitudes. These regions border cool oceans and experience plenty of precipitation all year long. The Mediterranean climate is similar to the Mediterranean basin climate. These regions have hot, dry summers and cool wet winters. These areas include South Australia, southwestern Africa, and central areas of Chile. The subarctic climate is very cold, continuous permafrost, and almost no precipitation.

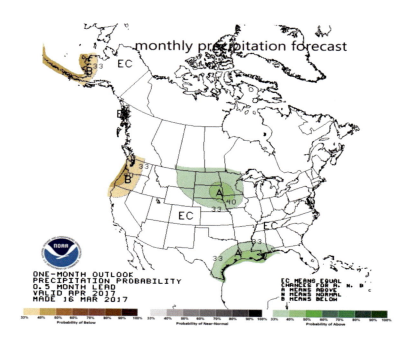

Chapter 14. Reading Weather Maps

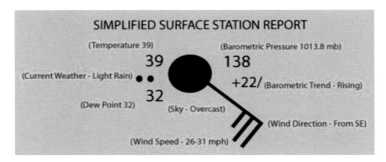

To summarize all of the data sent to central weather stations from various weather station locations, the creation of weather maps are used. Reports of precipitation, air pressure, wind speed, wind direction, temperature, dew point, cloud height, relative humidity, and previous weather changes within the last three hours, are among the data that is displayed on a weather map. Each day, at a particularly scheduled time, every six hours, all land weather stations and ships at sea report weather information. There are two types of weather maps: upper atmosphere charts, and surface charts. Some of the information is gathered from radiosondes which are weather balloons with electronic instruments on board that transmit the data every twelve hours. A computer plots all of the incoming data and prints this data on a printer called a *plotter*. All of the data gathered at the weather station is compressed into numbers and symbols about the size of a dime. Forecasting experts analyze the weather map and draw **isobars** to show lines of equal air pressure. Lines are close together show winds are strong. Where the lines are further apart will show that the winds are weak. The isobars are the lines drawn on the weather map to display areas of fronts and precipitation. From these charts, weather forecasters prepare their weather analysis to predict the weather. Lines of equal temperatures on the map are called **isotherms**. Predictions are made using mathematical formulas called numerical weather prediction (NWP) forecast. This process helps the meteorologist to make more accurate predictions.

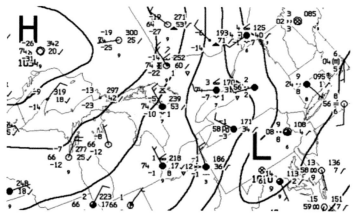

Courtesy of NOAA

Surface Weather Maps

The maps are a plotted map of the observations indicating fronts, temperature, and air pressure.

Cold fronts are shown as heavy solid lines. The lines contain triangles pointing to the direction that the cold front is heading.

Warm fronts are shown with standard lines with solid semi-circles attached to the line. The semi-circles point to the direction the warm front is heading.

Stationary fronts have triangles and semi-circles on opposite sides of the line. This indicates that the front has stalled and is not moving in either direction at the moment.

The occluded front is shown where cold air wraps around a low-pressure system. The occluded front is between the warm front and cold front. An occluded front extends from a strong cyclone. The occluded line will have alternating semicircles and triangles pointing in the same direction.

Isobars are contours of equal pressure. These solid lines are shown in **millibars**.

Centers for high and low pressure are indicated by the term "High" or "Low".

Surface winds spiral counterclockwise to indicate a cyclone (low-pressure area).

Area of a previous cyclone area is indicated with a chain of arrows and the center of a previous cyclone location is marked by a black square with a white cross.

Thick dashed lines indicate areas of a low-pressure area or low-pressure trough.

Surface winds spiral clockwise to indicate an anticyclone (high-pressure area).

Areas of Precipitation are marked by shaded areas.

Isotherms are lines of equal temperature at 32 degrees are shown with a thin dashed line.

Isotherms at 0 degrees F. are shown with a dotted line.

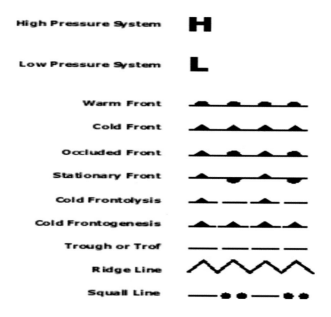

Courtesy of NOAA

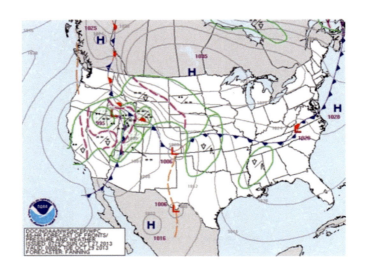

Chapter 15. Discoveries in Meteorology

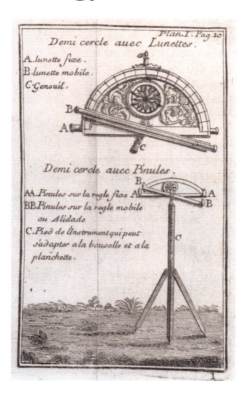

People in past did not have the modern technology that we have today in weather forecasting even though the weather has always an impact on people's lives in one form or another. Sailors and farmers had to find ways to predict the weather. Weather predictions made were using natural events as indicators. They would observe cloud formations, wave heights at sea, wind direction, dew on the plants for short-term predictions. They would use fuzzy caterpillars, bird flights, and other animal behavior observations for long-term weather predictions. Weather almanacs were used for years to assist people in predicting the weather. After World War II, serious studies of weather prediction had advanced and governments around the world have cooperated to advance further methods of weather prediction today.

Early beliefs of weather prediction:

1. The breastbone from a goose was used to tell whether there would be a bad winter. When the breastbone had dried, it would change color. If the dried bone was white, it would be predicted to be a mild winter. If the bone had dried purple, there would be a cold spring. If the *bone turned black, blue, or dark purple, it would be a harsh, cold winter. It was believed that the goose had conserved the natural body oils in its wings to protect itself from the cold.

2. Still celebrated today is Ground Hog's Day, February 2nd. German immigrants started this tradition while in Germany. German farmers would observe a badger as he emerged from hibernation. If the badger emerged on a sunny day, it would be scared by its shadow and the prediction would be six more weeks of winter. However, if it was a cloudy day and the badger did not see its shadow, the indication would be the start of spring. When the German immigrants came to America, they had noticed that there were few badgers in Pennsylvania. So, they substituted the groundhog as their weather predictor. To date, groundhog

predictions have been wrong about 70 percent of the time.

3. Have you ever heard the expression, "A ring around the Moon is a sign that rain will come"? What people are referring to is the view through high altitude cirrostratus clouds. The ice crystals within the clouds refract the Moon's light. The truth of the matter is cirrostratus clouds precede a warm front which is usually followed by turbulent weather, most likely in the form of rain.

4. "It smells like rain". This might be correct. Low-pressure is accompanied by rising air and precipitation. The earthy odor comes from the gases in the ground which diffuse with the air just before it rains.

5. Many people thought that bands on a wooly-bear caterpillar could be able to predict the severity of the coming winter. If the caterpillar black and reddish stripes were thick, the coming winter would be cold and harsh as it was believed. This belief obviously proved to be a false weather prediction method.

6. In 1857 a professor at the University of Utrecht, Buys Ballot, believed that "Standing with your back to the wind, low pressure is to the left, and high pressure is to the right in the Northern Hemisphere and the reverse in the Southern Hemisphere". Actually, the professor was right due to the Coriolis Effect.

Historic Discoveries in Meteorology

570 BC	Greek philosopher, Anaximenes of Miletus, stated that the air was the primary substance, and it changed to create wind, clouds, and rain.
140 BC	Han Ying test contained the first known reference to the hexagonal nature of snowflakes.
100 AD	Hero of Alexandria described experiments with air, including expanding air by heating it.
1304	Theodoric of Freiburg, concluded that water is responsible for the creation of a rainbow.
1586	Simon Stevinus concluded that the pressure of a liquid on a given surface depends on the height of the liquid and the area of the surface.
1644	Evangelista Torricelli and Vincenzo Viviani constructed the first barometer using mercury.
1654	The grand duke of Tuscany, Ferdinand II, invented the first sealed thermometer.
1662	Robert Boyle demonstrated that air pressure was not constant but changed with elevation.
1663	Robert Hooke showed that the height in a column of mercury would change before a storm. This pointed the way toward using the barometer in meteorology.

1709	Gabriel Daniel Fahrenheit constructed the first alcohol thermometer.
1714	Fahrenheit constructed a mercury thermometer with a scale that bears his name.
1735	George Hedley showed what is now called the Hedley cell, which models part of the Earth's wind circulation.
1823	John Frederic Daniell constructed the first comprehensive study of the atmosphere and trade winds.
1853	James Coffin discovered three distinct types wind zones in the Northern Hemisphere.
1863	Francis Galton used the term anticyclone and founded modern methods of mapping the weather.
1869	Cleveland Abbe sent out the first weather bulletins from the Cincinnati observatory where he worked.
1902	Teisserenc de Bort was the first to discover that the Earth's atmosphere has at least two layers, the troposphere and stratosphere.
1904	Vilhelm Bjerknes wrote the first scientific studies of weather forecasting.
1913	Charles Fabry discovered the ozonosphere.
1921	Vilhelm Bjerknes discovered that the atmosphere was made up of sharply different air masses.

1927	Rudolf Geiger founded the study of microclimatology.
1931	Auguste and Jean Felix Piccard were the first to ride a balloon to an altitude of 11 miles within a sealed gondola to protect themselves from the cold and thinness of the upper atmosphere.
1932	Car-Gustav Rossby first to diagram air mass properties.
1946	Vincent Schaefer discovered that carbon dioxide caused super-cooled water to turn to snow. He seeded clouds with dry ice causing the first artificial snowstorm.
1959	The U.S. Weather Bureau began the temperature-humidity index as a way of determining the comfort or discomfort of a hot day to humans.
1960	The United States launched the first weather satellite, The Television Infrared Observing Satellite 1 (TIROS 1).
1976	The first Geostationary Operations Environmental Satellite (GEOS) was launched
1984	Satellites launched by the National Oceanic and Atmospheric Administration (NOAA) started to measure new parameters in the atmosphere to determine weather and climate phenomena for meteorological models.

1989 Doppler radar used for weather forecasting.

1992 Ice cores from Greenland showed that during the last Ice Age, the climate changed dramatically over short periods. (As short as one to two years).

Notable Meteorologist

Abbe, Cleveland (1838-1916) American meteorologist who was the first to send out weather bulletins from the Cincinnati Observatory in 1869. He later became a scientific assistant in the first U.S. weather bureau, which was connected to the Army. He became head of the bureau after it had separated from the Army.

Anaximander (c. 610-546 B.C.) Greek philosopher and astronomer who believed that the wind was a natural phenomenon, not a divine one and that air is the basic principle of the universe.

Appleton, Sir Edward Victor (1892-1965) British physicist who discovered the layer of the atmosphere, called the ionosphere, is responsible for reflecting radio waves. The Appleton layer, or F-layer, of the atmosphere, is named in his honor.

Aratus (c.270 B.C.) Greek poet, who, around 270 B.C., wrote down in verse, thoughts on weather prediction, including a version of "Red sky in the morning, sailor take warning, red sky at night, sailor's delight".

Aristotle (384-322 B.C.) Greek philosopher and scientist who began the science of meteorology. Around 340 B.C., he published Meteorologica. This book was mostly wrong, but it summarized early ideas on meteorology and astronomy. He believed that everything in the universe was composed of four basic elements: earth, air, water, and fire.

Bergeron, Tor Harold Percival (1891-1971) Swedish meteorologist and cloud physicist who demonstrated that raindrops can form in the upper parts of clouds where there is little water, through the growth of ice crystals. This is called the Bergeron process in his honor.

Bjerknes, Jakob Aall Bonnevie (1897-1975) Norwegian meteorologist and son of Vilhelm who discovered that depressions form, develop, and decay along polar fronts. He also found large-scale atmospheric waves in the high westerly flow of the middle latitudes.

Bjerknes, Vilhelm Friman Koren (1862-1951) Norwegian meteorologist who explored the science of dynamical meteorology, worked on the origin and characteristic of depressions, and developed methods of the weather forecasting.

Bruckner, Edouard (1862-1927) German geographer and climatologist who studied the Alps' Pleistocene glaciation, and climatic fluctuations. He postulated that there was a 35-year period when the weather turned from damp and cold to dry and warm.

Buys Ballot, Christoph Hendrik Diederik (1817-1890) Dutch meteorologist who formulated the law for determining areas of low pressure based on observing the wind's direction.

Coriolis, Gustave-Gaspard (1792-1843) French physicist who in 1835 first described the curving deflection of winds caused by the Earth's rotation, now called the Coriolis Effect.

Dampier, William (1652-1715) English explorer and buccaneer, who first described the inner working so a tropical storm in a treatise entitled Discourse of Trade-Winds. He also was an expert in hydrology, pilotage, and winds, producing numerous navigator maps and charts.

Descartes, Rene du Perron (1596-1650) French philosopher, scientist, and mathematician who, along with important discoveries in other fields of science, explained the phenomenon of a rainbow formation.

Espy, James Pollard (1785-1860) American meteorologist who put together the first annual weather reports in 1843 and was a pioneer in weather forecasting.

Ferrel, William (1817-1891) American meteorologist who determined the law of atmospheric circulation, where winds are deflected to the right in the Northern Hemisphere and to the left in the Southern Hemisphere.

Fitzroy, Robert (1805-1865) British naval officer, hydrographer, and meteorologist, who commanded the HMS Beagle. This is the same ship that carried Charles Darwin. Fitzroy specialized in weather forecasting.

Galton, Francis Sir (1822-1911) British anthropologist and explorer who introduced the modern symbols for mapping the weather.

Hadley, George (1685-1768) English lawyer and climatologist who discovered that the additional heat from the sun in the equatorial regions was responsible for global wind patterns.

Howard, Luke (1772-1864) English amateur meteorologist who was the first to publish a classification system for clouds. His three primary classifications are still used, though 10 major cloud type is described in modern meteorology.

Koppen, Wladimir Peter (1846-1940) Russian born German climatologist and biologist who classified climatic types by annual temperature and precipitation and by relating them to the Earth's vegetation regions.

Piccard, Auguste (1884-1962) Swiss-born Belgian physicist who explored the upper stratosphere in an air balloon of his own design. In 1932, he launched a new cabin design for balloons to protect himself from the thin, cold upper atmosphere. He was the first human to enter the stratosphere, reaching an altitude of about 53,153 feet (16,201 meters). He also developed the deep decent bathyscaphe in 1948.

Pliny the Elder (Gaius Plinius Secundus) (23-79) Roman naturalist who believed that steady winds fall from the stars, or are created by the impact of the stars and the Earth as they travel in opposite directions

Redfield, William C. (1789-1857) American amateur meteorologist who studied hurricanes and was first to discover that the winds within the storms moved in a counterclockwise direction.

Rossby, Carl-Gustaf Arvid (1898-1957) Swedish born American meteorologist who discovered upper-level airwaves (called Rossby waves) and characteristics of air masses.

Teisserenc De Bort, Leon Philippe (1855-1913) French meteorologist who was the first to use unmanned balloons with instruments to measure the atmosphere. Through his balloon experiments, he discovered the stratosphere.

Thornthwaite, Charles Warren (1889-1963) American climatologist who classified climatic type by the moisture they contain. He developed the idea of global water balance.

Torricelli, Evangelista (1608-1647) Italian mathematician and physicist who is considered the father of hydrodynamics. He proposed an experiment that demonstrated that atmospheric pressure determined the height a fluid will rise in a tube when it is inserted into a container with the same liquid. This idea led to the development of the barometer.

Chapter 16. Terms

Absolute humidity – The total mass of water vapor within a certain amount of airspace. Usually, it refers to a cubic meter.

Adiabatic process – The way air temperature changes without removing or adding heat.

Advection fog – When fog occurs when warm humid air flows over cooler water or ground area.

Air mass – A body of air surrounded by cold or warm fronts. This body of air is at the lower level and maintains a constant water and temperature level.

Air pressure – Resulting from a collision of air molecules, it is the force of pressure exerted on any surface. Air pressure is measured with a barometer.

Air – The gases contained in the atmosphere.

Anabatic wind – A local wind warmed by the sun and moving upward over a slope.

Atmospheric pressure – Pressure created by the gravity on the air. Pressure decreases with increased altitude.

Barometer – an instrument used to measure atmospheric pressure.

Blizzard – A snowstorm that is combined with high winds.

Climate – A long-term weather effect constant over a period of time. This includes rainfall, temperature, winds, and air pressure.

Climatology – statistically studying the measurements of the atmosphere over a period of time. This area of meteorology relies on past records of a particular region.

Cloud seeding – The use of silver iodide and dry ice to create precipitation.

Cloud – When air is cooled to the dew point, and condensation has occurred, water droplets or ice crystals become suspended in the air.

Cold front – The boundary of a cooler air mass encroaching a warmer air mass.

Condensation – The process where water vapor turns into the liquid state.

Convection – The transfer of heat caused by the movement of warmer material.

Coriolis Effect – Due to the Earth's rotation, winds are forced to move toward the right in the northern hemisphere and to the left in the southern hemisphere.

Dew – The droplets of water that forms when the water vapor in the air condenses.

Dew point - The temperature where air becomes saturated and can no longer maintain water.

Diamond dust – Small airborne ice crystals reflecting sunlight.

Evaporation – Where water converts to a gas.

Flash flood – A sudden forceful flood due to a fast downfall of rain.

Fog – The bottom of a cloud that reaches the ground.

Front – Rain occurs when two air masses meet. Usually, they are two different temperatures and moisture levels.

Frost – When objects are below the freezing temperature, a layer of ice is formed.

Fulgurite – When lightning strikes dry sand, a glasslike piece of rock is formed.

Funnel cloud – The rotating extension of a cloud forming a tornado or waterspout.

Gale – A wind with speeds of 51 to 101 miles per hour.

Glory – The diffraction of light forming a colorful, circular halo.

Ground fog – Rising less than 200 feet, this type of fog forms over the cooled ground.

Gust – A sudden increase in wind. A gust is usually associated with squalls, thunderstorms, and high-pressure systems.

Hail – Pellets of ice that are usually formed in cumulonimbus clouds when the water droplets freeze and continue to fail and rise with the wind currents and re-freezing until they are too heavy to remain aloft.

Heat lightning – Lightning that occurs from cloud to cloud. Usually, this is a summer event.

Humidity – This is the water content in the air. Often referred to as relative humidity.

Inversion – Usually a stagnant weather condition, inversion occurs when a layer of cooler ground air remains beneath a layer of warmer air.

Isobars – Lines that connect layers of equal air pressure on a weather map.

*Katabatic wind – After sunset, the wind from the cooler air descends down a valley.

Lightning – An electrical discharge occurring in the atmosphere.

Precipitation – Water in the air that condenses and falls as rain, snow, ice, dew, or frost.

Relative humidity – The percentage of the amount of water that the air can hold at a certain temperature.

Rime – Also called sleet, this occurs when water droplets touch an object colder than the freezing point and the water turns to ice.

Saturation – When the air can hold its maximum amount of water at a given temperature and the water vapor condenses.

Sea smoke – the fog that occurs when warm air flows over a cooler body of water.

Shower – Snow or rain falling heavily or lightly at various intervals.

Storm surge – A rapid rise at coastlines due to strong winds.

Storm tracks – The path of a storm. Usually referred to its direction from one point toward another.

Sublimation – When ice changes to water vapor (a gas) or from water vapor to ice (a solid) without converting to liquid. Snow is formed by sublimation.

Temperature lapse rate – The rate that temperature decreases with height. Usually, the temperature drops three degrees every one thousand feet of altitude.

Temperature – The average kinetic energy (heat) measurement.

Trough – Usually a line of low pressure that runs north to south.

Virga – Water particles that fall to the ground but evaporate before it reaches the ground.

Warm front – A warm air mass approaching a cooler air mass.

Weather – Temporary changes in humidity, temperature, rainfall, and barometric pressure.

Wind – The movement of the air.

NOAA Terms –
Terminology and Weather Symbols

FRONTS

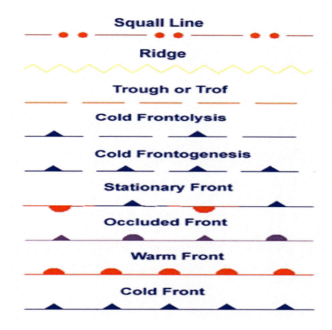

Cold front

-The leading edge of a relatively colder air mass which separates two air masses in which the gradients of temperature and moisture are maximized.

In the northern hemisphere winds ahead of the front will be southwest and shift into the northwest with the frontal passage.

Frontogenesis
- The formation of a front occurs when two adjacent air masses with different densities and temperatures meet and strengthen the discontinuity between the air masses . It occurs most frequently over continental land areas such as over the Eastern US when the air mass moves out over the ocean. It is the opposite of frontolysis.

Frontolysis

-The weakening or dissipation of a front occurs when two adjacent air masses lose contrasting properties such as the density and temperature.

It is the opposite of frontogenesis.

Occluded front

- The union of two fronts, formed as a cold front overtakes a warm front or quasi-stationary front refers to a cold front occlusion.

When a warm front overtakes a cold front or quasi-stationary front the process is termed a warm front occlusion.

These processes lead to the dissipation of the front in which there is no gradient in temperature and moisture.

Ridge

- An elongated area of relatively high pressure that is typically associated with an anti-cyclonic wind shift.

Stationary front

- A front that has not moved appreciably from its previous analyzed position.

Trough

- [Trof], an elongated area of relatively low pressure that is typically associated with a cyclonic wind shift.

Warm front

- The leading edge of a relatively warmer surface air mass which separates two distinctly different air masses.

The gradients of temperature and moisture are maximized in the frontal zone.

Ahead of a typical warm front in the northern hemisphere, winds are from the southeast and behind the front winds will shift to the southwest.

LOW & HIGH-PRESSURE SYSTEMS AND MISCELLANEOUS KEY TERMS USED

 Low Pressure

 High Pressure

Low-pressure with a number such as <u>99</u> means <u>999</u> mb and with <u>03</u> means <u>1003</u> mb. High-pressure with a number such as <u>25</u> means <u>1025</u> mb.

Extratropical low

- A low-pressure center which refers to a migratory frontal cyclone center and higher latitudes. Tropical cyclones occasionally evolve into extratropical lows losing tropical characteristics and become associated with frontal discontinuity.

Low-pressure

- An area of low-pressure identified with counterclockwise circulation in the northern hemisphere and clockwise in the southern hemisphere.

Also, defined as a cyclone.

High-pressure

- An area of higher pressure identified with a clockwise circulation in the northern hemisphere and a counterclockwise circulation in the southern hemisphere.

Also, defined as an anticyclone.

New

- The term "NEW" may be used in lieu of a forecast track position of a high or low pressure center when the center is expected to form by a specific time. For example, a surface analysis may depict a 24-hour position of a new low-pressure center with an "X" at the 24-hour position followed by the term "NEW", the date and time in UTC which indicates the low is expected to form by 24 hours.

Rapidly intensifying

- Indicates an expected rapid intensification of a cyclone with surface pressure expected to fall by at least 24 millibars (mb) within 24 hours.

Station plot

coding used with the surface preliminary analysis or for a list of "present weather" symbols.

Weather Parameter	Weather Symbol Decoded
Station ID	KPZH
Temperature (fahrenheit or Celsius)	70 degree F
Present weather	R thunderstorm
Dewpoint temperature (Fahrenheit or Celsius)	68 degree F
Wind speed, direction, sky cover	SSW 25 kt overcast
Station Pressure (MB)	048 = 1004.8 MB
3 hour pressure tendency	-7 \ = -0.7 mb pressure decrease with steady pressure fall
optional wave height (feet or meter)	11 ft
Sea Surface Temperature (Fahrenheit or Celsius)	75 degrees F

Squall
- A sudden wind increase characterized by a duration of minutes and followed by a sudden decrease in winds.

Wind speed & Direction

NE 2 KT   NE 5 KT   NE 10 KT   NE 15 KT   NNE 45 KT   N 50 KT   N 65 KT

FOG

======   **Light Fog**

======   **Heavy Fog**

Fog

-Over the marine environment, the term fog refers to visibility greater than or equal to 1/2 NM and less than 3 NM.

Fog is the visible aggregate of minute water droplets suspended in the atmosphere near the surface.

Dense Fog

-Over the marine environment, the term dense fog refers to visibility less than 1/2 NM. Fog is the visible aggregate of minute water droplets suspended in the atmosphere near the surface. Usually, dense fog occurs when air that is lying over a warmer surface such as the Gulf Stream is spread across a colder water surface and the lower layer of the air mass is cooled below its dew point.

Fog is lifting

Sea Fog

- Common advection fog caused by transport of moist air over a cold body of water.

FREEZING SPRAY and ICE EDGE

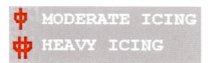

Freezing spray

- Spray in which super-cooled water droplets freeze upon contact with exposed objects below the freezing point of water.

It usually develops in areas with winds of at least 25 knots.

Categories of Freezing Spray/Icing

Light	Moderate	Heavy
Less than 0.7 cm/hr.	0.7 cm/hr. to less than or equal to 2.0 cm/hr.	Greater than 2.0 cm/hr.
Less than	0.3 ins/hr. to less than	Greater than

| 0.3 ins/hr. | or equal to 0.8 ins/hr. | 0.8 ins/hr. |

Ice Edge

- Represented by a blue dotted line and is defined by the National Ice Center.

It depicts the extent of ice coverage 10% or greater.

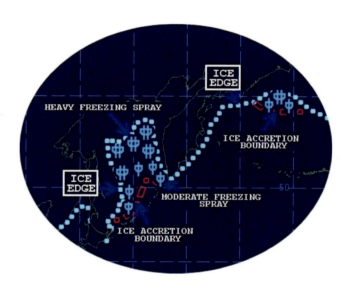

CONVENTIONS USED WITH WARNINGS FOR EXTRATROPICAL SYSTEMS

Extratropical Systems

Complex gale/storm

-An area in which gale/storm force winds are

forecast or are occurring, but in which more than one center is the generating these winds.

Developing Gale

-Refers to an extratropical low or an area in which gale force winds of 34 knots (39 mph) to 47 knots (54 mph) are "expected" by a certain time period. On surface analysis charts, a "DEVELOPING GALE" label indicates gale force winds within the next 24 hours. When the label is used on the 48-hour surface forecast and 96 hour surface forecast charts, gale force winds are expected to develop by 72 hours and 120 hours, respectively.

Developing Storm

-Refers to an extratropical low or an area in which storm force winds of 48 knots (55 mph) to 63 knots (73 mph) are "expected" by a certain time period.

On surface analysis charts, a "DEVELOPING

STORM" label indicates storm force winds forecast within the next 24 hours. When the label is used on the 48-hour surface and 96-hour surface charts, storm force winds are expected to develop by 72 hours and 120 hours, respectively.

Developing Hurricane Force

-Refers to an extratropical low or an area in which hurricane force winds of 64 knots (74 mph) or higher are "expected" by a certain time period. On surface analysis charts, a "DEVELOPING HURRICANE FORCE" label indicates hurricane force winds forecast within the next 24 hours. When the label is used on the 48-hour surface and 96-hour surface charts, hurricane force winds are expected to develop by 72 hours and 120 hours, respectively.

Gale

- Refers to an extratropical low or an area of

sustained surface winds (averaged over a ten minute period, momentary gusts may be higher) of 34 knots (39 mph) to 47 knots (54 mph).

Storm

- Refers to an extratropical low or an area of sustained winds (averaged over a ten minute period, momentary gusts may be higher) of 48 knots (55 mph) to 63 knots (73 mph).

Hurricane Force

- Refers to an extratropical low or an area of sustained winds (averaged over a ten minute period, momentary gusts may be higher) in excess of 64 knots or higher (74 mph).

Small Craft Advisory

- Refers to areas within the coastal waters with sustained winds of 18 knots (21 mph) to 33 knots (38 mph).

Heavy Freezing Spray

-Spray in which super cooled water droplets freeze upon contact with exposed objects below the freezing point of water at the rate of greater than 2 cm/hr. It usually develops in areas with winds of at least 25knots.

CONVENTIONS USED WITH WARNINGS FOR TROPICAL SYSTEMS

Tropical Systems

Hurricane

- A tropical cyclone with closed contours, a strong and very pronounced circulation, and one-minute maximum sustained surface winds 64 knots (74 mph) or greater.

A system is called a hurricane over the North Atlantic, Gulf of Mexico, North Pacific East of the dateline, and the South Pacific East of 160E.

Intertropical Convergence Zone

- (ITCZ) The region where the northeasterly and southeasterly trade winds converge, forming an often continuous band of clouds or thunderstorms near the equator.

Post-Tropical

- A cyclone that no longer possesses sufficient tropical characteristics to be considered a tropical cyclone.

Post-tropical cyclones can continue carrying intense rainfalls and high winds. [Note that former tropical cyclones that have become fully extra-tropical, as well as remnant lows, are two classes of post-tropical cyclones. The term "post-tropical" is predominantly a convenient communications term--to permit the ongoing use of the storm name.]

Tropical cyclone

- A non-frontal, warm-core, low-pressure system of synoptic scale, developing over tropical or subtropical waters with definitely organized convection (thunderstorms) and a well-defined surface wind circulation.

Tropical depression

- A tropical cyclone with one or more closed isobars and a one-minute max sustained surface wind of less than 34 knots (39 mph).

Tropical storm

- A tropical cyclone with closed isobars and a one minute max sustained surface wind of 34 knots (39 mph) to 63 knots (73 mph).

Typhoon

- Same as a hurricane with exception of the geographical area. A tropical cyclone with closed contours, a strong and very pronounced circulation , and one-minute maximum sustained surface winds of 64 knots (74 mph) or greater.

A system is defined as a typhoon over the North Pacific West of the dateline.

NOTE: It can be difficult to determine the central pressures of tropical depressions, tropical storms, and hurricanes/typhoons and at times no estimates or measurements are provided by a hurricane or typhoon specialist.

An estimate of central pressure may be provided over the Atlantic. Otherwise, an XXX is used in place of actual or estimated pressures associated with these systems and an XX is used for forecast central pressure.

SEAS

Combined seas
-The combination of both wind waves and swell which is generally referred to as "seas".

Primary swell direction
- Prevailing direction of swell propagation.

Significant wave height
- The average height (trough to crest) of the 1/3rd highest waves. An experienced observer will most frequently report the highest 1/3rd of the waves observed.

The generation of waves on water results not in a single wave height but in a spectrum of waves distributed from the smallest capillary waves to larger waves. Within this spectrum, there is a finite possibility of each of the wave heights to occur with the largest waves being the least likely. The wave height most commonly observed and the forecast is the significant wave height. This is defined as the average of the one third highest waves.

The random nature of waves implies that individual waves can be substantially higher than the significant wave height. In fact, observations and theory show that the highest individual waves in a typical storm with typical duration to be approximately two times the significant wave height. Some reported rogue waves are well within this factor of two envelopes.

Waves higher than roughly twice the significant wave height fall into the category of extreme or rogue waves.

Swell

- Wind waves that have moved out of their fetch or wind generation area.

Waves generated by swell exhibit a regular and longer period than wind waves.

MISCELLANEOUS TERMINOLOGY

Coastal Waters

- Includes the area from a line approximating the

mean high water along the mainland or island as far out as sixty nautical miles including the bays, harbors, and sounds.

High Seas

- That portion of the Atlantic and Pacific oceans which extends off the Western and Eastern US coasts and extends to 35W in the Atlantic ocean and to 160E in the Pacific Ocean.

The area includes both the coastal and offshore waters.

Offshore waters

- That portion of oceans, gulfs, and seas beyond coastal waters extending to a specified distance from the coastline, to a specified depth contour, or covering an area defined by a specific latitude and longitude points.

Chapter 17. Greatest Annual Snowfalls in the U.S.

Location	Inches	Centimeters
Blue Canyon, CA	240.8	611.6
Marquette, MI	126.0	320.0
Sault St. Marie, MI	116.4	295.7
Caribou, ME	111.5	283.2
Syracuse, NY	110.5	280.7
Mount Shasta, CA	104.9	266.4
Lander, WY	103.9	263.9
Muskegon, MI	98.4	249.9
Sexton Summit, OR	97.8	248.4
Flagstaff, AZ	96.4	244.9

Although the weather can be an extreme problem at times, there are some areas of recreation that people enjoy. Skiing is one of them. Can you name other enjoyable winter activities?

Chapter 18. Projects and badge requirements

Although some school systems briefly cover meteorology within their earth science curriculum, many youth organizations include weather as a valid part of their program. This particular meteorology badge requirement for one youth group embarks on several fun projects that induce the learning of weather in an interesting method.

Project requirements:

1. Define meteorology, explain what weather and climate are about. Explain how weather affects fisherman, farmers, pilots, and the construction industry. Explain how weather forecasting is important to each profession.
2. Name five dangerous weather conditions. Explain safety rules when outdoors. Explain the difference between a severe weather watch and a weather warning. Discuss the safety rules with your family.
3. Explain what occurs with a high-pressure and low-pressure system. Which is associated with good weather and which is associated with the poor weather? Draw a cross-section of a warm front and a cold front. Show the locations of warm air and cold air. Show the frontal slope and the types of clouds related to each type of front and show the location of precipitation.
4. Explain what causes wind, how rain, lightning, and hail are formed.

5. Show and describe clouds in the low, middle, and upper levels of the atmosphere. Explain how they are associated with each type of weather event.
6. Draw a diagram of the water cycle and label its major processes.
7. Explain some possible human actions that may alter the environment, climate, and people.
8. Explain the tilt of the Earth's axis and how it can determine the climate of a region around the equator, at the poles, and at the areas between the equator and the poles.
9. Do one of the following:
    a. Make one of the following weather instruments: a rain gauge, wind vane, anemometer, or hygrometer. Using your instrument, keep a daily weather log for one week. Include the weather statistics from the news. Record the information at the same time each day. Compare the accuracy of your findings and the news reports. Include in your report the temperature, types of clouds, and precipitation. Note any morning frost or dew.
    b. Find out what types of weather conditions are most dangerous to your community and how warnings are giving to the community. Contact a weather station, radio or television weather forecaster, a meteorologist, or an agricultural extension service office.
10. Do one of the following:

a. Give a talk for at least five minutes to a group explaining the outdoor safety rules in the event of lightning, tornadoes, or flash floods.
b. Read articles about acid rain and give a prepared talk of at least five minutes to a group.
11. Discover career-related opportunities in the weather-related field. Find out about the training and education required for each position.

Fun Projects: Build a Weather Station with Five Instruments

1. <u>Build a Wind Vane</u>

Needed Materials:

_ Strong Scissors   _ Saw   _Glue

_ Mallet _ Hammer _ Thick metal washers

_ Drill _ 2 or 3=inch nail _ 12-inch piece of wood (1/2 inch thick)

_ 3-foot garden stick (1 inch thick) _ Aluminum pie tin

Wind Vane instructions:

First, select a good location where it will not be in the way of anyone and the wind vane will have access to the wind in all directions. Using the mallet, drive the stick into the ground.

Second: With a saw, cut a half inch slot into the 12-inch piece of wood, at both ends.

Third: Drill a hole down the shaft of the garden stick and drill a hole in the center of the 12-inch piece of wood at the center. Place the washer over each hole. Both washers should be facing each other.

Four: Cut the aluminum pie plate in the shape of an arrowhead and another piece in the shape of an arrow tail. Glue the arrowhead to one slot in the 12-inch piece of wood and the tail at the other end. The piece of wood should rotate freely.

2. The Outdoor Thermometer –

Place the outdoor thermometer in a shaded area away from direct sunlight and wind.

weather thermometer

3. Build an Anemometer –

Needed Materials:

- Tape
- a Marker
- 2 very long plastic straws or light weight wooden reeds.
- Long straight pin
- Hole punch
- 5 plastic or foam cups
- freshly sharpened Pencil or awl

Instructions to build the anemometer:

Note: Using Styrofoam cups maybe easier to work with, however these cups disintegrate very quickly. Be creative and find something that is very light, easy to put holes into it, and will cup the wind.

First: Mark a number one on one cup and set it aside.

Second: Select a cup and punch holes through the sides near the top of the cup. You will be inserting the straws directly into the cup so that the two straws intersect each other. Make sure that one pair of holes is slightly lower than the second set so that the straw won't collide with each other.

Third: Using the same cup, poke a hole through the bottom. Find the center first.

Fourth: Insert the two straws into the cup so that they intersect each other. Insert the pencil through the bottom of the cup until the eraser part touches the first straw. Tape the straws in place.

Fifth: Push the straight pin through both straws and into the eraser part of the pencil. Make sure that the cup can turn freely.

Sixth: Punch ONE hole in each remaining cup. Mount the cups on the straw so that each cup bottom is pointing in a different direction. Make sure that none of the cup bottoms are facing each other.

To record wind speed, simply count the number of revolutions the anemometer makes in one minute. One revolution would be every time the 'marked one' cup passes a point.

4. <u>Build a Hygrometer</u> -

The purpose of a hygrometer is to determine the amount of water vapor that is the air. To put it simply, it requires two thermometers. One will have a wick that is constantly wet. The number that you are seeking is the difference in the readings of the two thermometers.

Using a milk carton or container, attach both thermometers to the container. For one of the thermometers, cut a slit about two or three inches from the bottom of the container. Using a new shoelace, cut six inches of the lace. Place one end of the piece of lace over the bulb at the bottom of one of the thermometers and the other end of the shoelace in through the slit near the bottom of the container. Fill the carton or container with water, up to the slot.

The dry bulb thermometer will give the air temperature. The wet bulb thermometer will render a lower temperature. This occurs because evaporation of water in the wick will lower the temperature. To calculate the humidity, subtract the difference of the wet bulb thermometer from the dry bulb thermometer reading. Note the resulting number and use the chart below to deduce the relative humidity in the air.

Relative Humidity Chart –

Difference	30	40	50	60	70	80	90	100
1	88	92	93	94	95	96	96	
2	77	84	87	89	90	92	92	
3	67	76	80	84	86	87	89-	
4	57	68	74	78	81	83	85-	
6	37	58	62	68	72	76	78	80
8	17	38	50	58	64	68	71	74
10	23	39	49	56	61	65	68	
12	9	28	40	48	54	59	62	
14		17	31	41	48	53	57	
16		7	23	34	41	47	52	

18	14	27	35	42	47
20	7	20	30	37	42
22		14	24	32	38
24		7	19	27	33
26		1	14	22	29
28			9	18	25
30			4	14	21

5. <u>Build a Rain Gage</u> -

A rain gage is an instrument that is simple to make. You need to obtain a clear glass or plastic tube. An olive jar will do. Make a ruler or numbered scale using the ruler. Mark your scale in half-inch increments and tape it to the outside of the jar. You should be able to read the markings through the side of the tube. Set a good-sized funnel over the opening of the tube. Cut both sides of a tuna can and place that over the funnel to be used as a splash guard.

Compass

Compass – Use a compass to verify wind direction.

Activity: Practice analyzing weather maps. Look closely at this surface weather map and read what you find. Make a forecast for areas on the map.

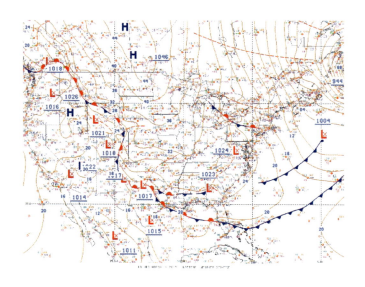

Thank you for reading WEATHER by Jack Fleming. I hope that you've enjoyed this book. Pass on your knowledge

208

to others and please recommend this and other books by Jack Fleming to everyone that you know.

May all of <u>your</u> weather be happy and bright.

THE END

Made in the USA
Middletown, DE
15 February 2023

24911572R00117